Palgrave Insights into Apocalypse Economics

Series Editor
Richard Westra, Centre for Macau Studies
University of Macau, Macau, China

This series is set to become the lodestone for critical Marxist and related Left scholarship on the raft of apocalyptic tendencies enveloping the global economy and society. Its working premise is that neoliberal policies from the 1980s not only failed to rejuvenate capitalist prosperity lost with the demise of the post-Second World War 'golden age' economy but in fact have generated a widening spectrum of pathologies that threaten humanity itself. At the most fundamental level the series cultivates state of the art critical political economic analysis of the crises, recessionary, deflationary and austerity conditions that have beset the world economy since the global meltdown of 2008–2009. However, though centered on work that critically explores global propensities for devastating financial convulsions, ever-widening inequalities and economic marginalisation due to information technologies, robotised production and low wage outsourcing, it seeks to draw on exacerbating factors such as climate change and global environmental despoliation, corrupted food systems and land-grabbing, rampant militarism, cyber crime and terrorism, all together which defy mainstream economics and conventional political policy solutions.

For critical Marxist and related Left scholars the series offers a non-sectarian outlet for academic work that is hard-hitting, inter/trans-disciplinary and multiperspectival. Its readership draws in academics, researchers, students, progressive governmental and non-governmental actors and the academically-informed public.

More information about this series at
http://www.palgrave.com/gp/series/15867

Carlos Manuel Sánchez Ramírez

Knowledge Capitalism and State Theory

A "Space-Time" Approach Explaining Development Outcomes in the Global Economy

palgrave
macmillan

Carlos Manuel Sánchez Ramírez
Faculty of Economics
National Autonomous University
of Mexico
Mexico City, Mexico

ISSN 2523-8108 ISSN 2523-8116 (electronic)
Palgrave Insights into Apocalypse Economics
ISBN 978-3-030-71410-9 ISBN 978-3-030-71411-6 (eBook)
https://doi.org/10.1007/978-3-030-71411-6

Cover illustration: Dina Belenko/Alamy Stock Photo

This Palgrave Macmillan imprint is published by the registered company Springer Nature Switzerland AG
The registered company address is: Gewerbestrasse 11, 6330 Cham, Switzerland

Contents

List of Figures

List of Diagrams

List of Tables

CHAPTER 1

Introduction: Revisiting State Theory in Knowledge Capitalism After Markets Failure and Pandemic Crisis Through a Space–Time Approach

The global financial–productive crisis of 2008 questioned the theoretical capability of the neoclassical synthesis and its statistical–econometric toolkit to understand and interpret contemporary capitalism from its static equilibrium approach, a situation that tends to deepen because of the economic impact of the COVID-19 global pandemic. This makes it necessary to recognize the long-term cyclical nature of capitalism in time, as well as its scalar differentiation in space in order to move toward its analysis as a system in constant dynamic imbalance.

This recognition of time and space dimensions places this work in terms of time in the emergence and unfolding of a new phase of development or Knowledge Capitalism during the eighties of the last century onward, characterized by cognitive and creative labor capabilities valorization as a great achievement for capitalism to overcome its historical crisis. Meanwhile, the deployment of electronics and telecommunications technological revolution endowed this phase of development with an unprecedented capacity for territorial expansion on global and virtual scales.

International financial capital flows and venture capitals in particular provided the necessary boost to incorporate emerging technologies into

C. M. Sánchez Ramírez, *Knowledge Capitalism and State Theory*, Palgrave Insights into Apocalypse Economics,
https://doi.org/10.1007/978-3-030-71411-6_1

the scope of production at the beginning of this phase of development. However, productive and financial capitals have had a divergent relationship in the new century, in such a way that under Atlantic neoliberal development pathway, a process of global economic structure molding shaped by financial capital has prevailed.

The superstructural projection of this process resulted in the vanishing of the old Fordist–Keynesian Welfare State, as the most efficient agent for social resources distribution in favor of the market, intensifying the struggle between the market and the State to represent the social. Global financial crisis of 2008 or "market failure" and its spread through international financial markets, digitally interconnected by the boom in telecommunications and the production of virtual space, expresses capitalism's immanent instability as a result of its cyclical nature and questions the effectiveness of the market.

Moreover, among the main arguments in favor of an urgent need for the return of the State to promote economic growth and development are first the uncertainty about the capacity of the United States and Western Europe as developed regions, to recover and increase the pace of their economic growth after the pandemic crisis; second, the best performance of China to manage financial and health crises, its transition from an outside growth model to one based on the strengthening of its domestic market and its attempt to shift the epicenter of the global economy from the Atlantic to the Pacific via the Belt and Road Initiative and as well as the consequences that those processes will have for the developing world, mainly Latin America and Africa.

Furthermore, there is a certain degree of skepticism about the implementation of "innovative" instruments of monetary policy to combat chronic problems in the European Union economy, such as deflation, unemployment and stagnation of economic growth. Such is the case of quantitative easing, meaning the creation of new money by central banks to purchase government bonds, with the main objective of lowering long-term interest rates. The expected effects of this reduction are the encouragement of commercial banks, the increase in companies' share values and the creation of a climate of confidence for businesses, mechanisms that would eventually result in the reactivation of the economy. However, in the case of the United States, these extraordinary resources have had a limited impact in the long term of productive capital as a whole as shown by the level of the industrial profit rate, which in 2019 was practically the same as in 2009, one year after the financial crisis.

Latin America is no stranger to looming challenges. Significant economic growth rates at the beginning of the new century resulted from high prices of raw materials driven by the boom in Chinese exports to the rest of the world. But the economic stagnation of the United States and the European Union after the financial crisis of 2008 first and the economic impact of the pandemic crisis later, which hastens China's turn toward its domestic market and to its closest area of influence in East Asia, marked the closing of the extraordinary income cycle for Latin America.

These exceptional conditions would have made it easier for governments identified with the electoral left in South America to carry out attempts in the search for post-neoliberal development pathways, moving away differently from the reforms synthesized in the Washington Consensus, with which the region had a significant degree of commitment in the nineties of the twentieth century. However, the end of the expansionary cycle with high prices of raw materials and the insufficiency of the neo-developmental experiences in Brazil and Argentina meant a wasted decade for the economic structure transformation of the region. So, new attempts of successful insertion into current phase of development link directly to the capacity of the States to consolidate alternative development pathways to neoliberalism.

This contemporary global scenario characterized by economic stagnation and uncertainty makes relevant the revisit and discussion of the theory of the State and its role in economic development in Knowledge Capitalism from a space–time perspective, taking into account the praxis and specific weights of social relations. This work aims to contribute to the discussion on the role of the State as a time–space *constructum*, to study and understand national development modalities that overcame the condition of backwardness. These lessons will light the path of post-neoliberalism in Latin America, as well as post-COVID-19 pandemic new World Order resulting from the contrast of predominant development pathways on a global scale.

The work consists of two theoretical chapters, three case studies, one of contrast between the case studies and one more of concluding remarks, as follows. The second one, *the socio–space–time relativity of the State* recognizes that Marx does not properly develop a theory of the State, but it can be developed from the alienation of capitalism theory enriched with the theoretical contributions of other authors. While Lenin emphasizes the coercive aspect of the State, meaning an instrument of oppression resulted from capital–labor social conflict, Gramsci underlines the exercise of consensus by the ruling classes over the subaltern ones to justify and maintain their rule, giving rise to the realization of Hegemony armored of coercion or political society plus civil society as a full State.

In the State economic scope, Gerschenkron argues that development of the first European backward countries could not follow a linear process such as those already developed, but rather from the specificities of backwardness with respect to the advanced countries, thus, giving place to a development from time leaps, strengthening the character of the State as a representative of the social, not only in the political but also in the economic sphere. As development of backward nations is not linear, a sequence of imbalances that induce economic policies and investments that open new stages of development as Hirschman suggests should be seek in regions like in Latin America. Furthermore, Evans proposes an embedded autonomy of the State to promote an international competitive industrial capacity as the way East Asian developmental States arose in the global economic hierarchy.

Thus, the specificities of the State's action to overcome the condition of backwardness are relative to the development of capitalism over time and entail a certain differentiation in space. Marx recognizes not only the cyclical character of capitalism when explaining the short or industrial cycle in *Das Kapital* but also its expansive territorial tendency, formulating a principle of space–time relativity of the system. However, are recent theorists such as Henri Lefebvre and David Harvey, who conceive space as a process and a medium that implies conditions inherited from the past and is the result of social relations, breaking with the common fetishized idea of it by considering it as a mere container of social relationships.

Coinciding with Gramsci's concepts of restricted and full State, Neil Brenner differentiates between analytical and integral State space in order to address the spatiality of the State, its regulatory strategies and its sociopolitical conflicts. This set of theoretical contributions represent a step forward to formulate a State theory relative to its space–time dimensions, in order to elaborate the political foundation of the State to undertake an economic and spatial development pathway from a situation of backwardness in a certain stage of capitalism development meaning as State's time dimension as developed in Chapter 3.

Chapter 3, *Long-Term Cyclicality of Capitalism as State Time Dimension* explores contributions of the long-term cyclicality of capitalism system such as Kondratiev's long cycles, Mandel's long waves, Schumpeter's economic development and Perez's technological waves, in order to contextualize Gramsci's phase of development concept. The last emerges in a historic crisis situation of contradiction between productive forces and social relations of production, giving rise to a new phase of development from the articulation between technological changes with social construction, projecting a new historic solution to social conflict that includes a State form.

The structural construction of Knowledge Capitalism as the present phase of development founds on microprocessor and software invention that radically transformed machine–tools, and its articulation with a new solution to antagonism and social conflict that step forward toward the immediate recognition of the individual as a social being through cognitive and creative labor force capabilities valorization. An industrial revolution arose from the previous conjunction, having electronic and telecommunication technologies as driving industrial branches reconfiguring intra-industrial and global division of labor.

The evolving economic–structure of the new phase of development emerged mainly from the Atlantic–hegemonic neoliberal development pathway which brought the formation of a new Historic Bloc in the United States under the Hegemony of Schumpeterian entrepreneurs that projected the market as the most efficient agent for the distribution of available social resources. However, different development pathways emerged based under Knowledge Capitalism economic structure through distinctive State–spatial formations that overcame backwardness as the Nordic and Asian development pathways. Financial–productive global crisis and COVID-19 pandemic crisis highlight the distinctive features of these State forms and their development pathways in contrast to the declining neoliberalism, shaping the way to a post-pandemic new World Order as discussed in the following chapters.

Based on the theoretical–conceptual framework addressed in Chapters 2 and 3, the following three present study cases of national experiences centered in the economic–spatial action of the State to configure specific development pathways based on the hegemonic capacity of its Historic Blocs to transit to the new phase of development. Chapters 4 and 5 study Finland and China, respectively, to continue with Brazil and Argentina in Chapter 6. Meanwhile, Chapter 7 proposes a theoretical–analytical discussion on the main trends of predominant development pathways clash toward a global hegemonic rearrangement.

Therefore, Chapter 4, *Finland, the Innovate State* addresses the case of the Nordic country that even in the mid-twentieth century was in a backwardness situation, with the predominance of a forest economy and under the continuous siege of a great power such as the former Soviet Union. These conditions would radically change during the second half of the last century, to position Finland as one of the most competitive and innovative nations at the dawn of the twenty-first century. The Innovate State resulted from a strong hegemonic power of the Finnish industrial bourgeoisie within the Historic Bloc, with sufficient convening capacity through Gramscian institutions such as social democracy, cooperatives and education, to integrate the rest of the classes and social groups into a project of future around a society of innovation and learning.

Chapter 5, *China: The Visible Hand of the State* addresses one of the most paradigmatic cases of the new century, that of a great emerging power under the economic structure of the present phase of development, currently in a position of dispute with the United States in its International System of States Hegemony. The chapter presents the Chinese State form as a Competitive State resulted from a reconfigured Historic Bloc after the exhaustion of the Maoist mass line that demonstrated its failure as a development pathway during the Great Leap Forward with a drop of more than twenty percentage points of gross domestic product.

The moderate fraction of the Chinese Communist Party (CCP) led this rearrangement after Mao's death, spreading within the bureaucracy of the Party first, and toward the rest of society later, including the strategic Chinese bourgeoisie settled in the Asian basin or Greater China, a pragmatic development pathway under a new Hegemony summarized in the premise *economy in command*. A set of economic reforms initiated in the agricultural, industrial, commercial and financial spheres, allowing the transition of China from statism to mercantile capitalism, including a State spatial selectivity where the establishment of Special Economic Zones played a fundamental role.

Thus, from a strong hegemonic capacity within the Historic Bloc resulting in an active economic–spatial action of its Competitive State, China integrated into Knowledge Capitalism achieving significant rates of economic growth. This based on a development pathway of exports promotion started in the lower links of the global production networks, but moving toward high cognitive value added, in transition to economic growth based on domestic market, in an attempt to shift the epicenter of the global economy from the Atlantic to the Pacific. The uncertain economic recovery of the developed world after financial and pandemic crises accelerates this process configuring a post-pandemic realignment of global Hegemony.

Chapter 6, *Brazil and Argentina, Hegemonic Crisis, Neo-Developmental State and Wasted Decade,* approaches to Latin America national experiences in their recent effort to search for alternative development pathways to neoliberalism, after a strong commitment with it during the last decade of the twentieth century. The chapter presents the three stages of imports substitution industrialization strategy during Fordist–Keynesian phase of development as the result of social struggle within the Historic Bloc, placing special interest in the Passive Revolution periods when the State promoted national industrialization above the interests of ruling classes by representing the social interest to boost development under national premises.

This allows glimpsing the Hegemonic crisis within the Historic Blocs of both countries, meaning the industrial bourgeoisies' inability to lead a development project, as well as the ability of the agro-exporting bourgeoisies to invalidate and neutralize the economic–spatial action of the State to undertake backwardness. Broad social mobilizations that took place at the dawn of the new century opened an opportunity for structural change. Taking advantage of the export boom of raw materials linked to its strong demand from China, governments identified with left parties achieved visible social progress by implementing redistributive policies, but still insufficient to overcome backwardness. This configured a wasted decade for neo-developmental States in Brazil and Argentina and the establishment of bizarre forms of neoliberalism during last years, meaning new challenges for the region in the financial and post-pandemic crises world.

Chapter 7, *Post-pandemic COVID-19 World Order: Decline of Neoliberalism and Strike Back of the State? A Reading from Gramsci* combines the study of development modalities addressed in the previous chapters in the framework of an ongoing crisis situation in the time lapse between the financial–pandemic crises. Gramsci's theoretical lens and the pandemic's first hit empirical evidence together with post-financial crisis health data let gauging the decline of neoliberalism through the exhaustion of market as the most efficient agent to solve the social conflict and the rise of the State as a more effective social representative to manage both crises.

Spatially, the analysis considers fifteen leading and following countries of the studied development pathways. Meanwhile, two variables show the connection link between the global productive financial crisis of 2008 and the State's ability to manage the current health crisis caused by COVID-19 pandemic. The first is the full State, measured by the expansion or reduction of the State's health expenditure, as well as its capability to constrain market action especially those of private health insurances. The second is the restricted State, meaning its capability to minimize SARS–CoV–2 lethality. Both variables' spatial behavior during the time lapse results in a State–market–financial–pandemic–crisis vector, allowing outlining the main trends of the predominant development pathways in the post-pandemic World Order.

Finally, Chapter 8, *Conclusions: New Cold War as Post-pandemic COVID-19 World Order?*, addresses final notes on the convenience of changing the study perspective of current global economic–political dynamics in Knowledge Capitalism considering a space–time approach in the face of the limits of classical analysis to explain it. Thus, the concluding remarks emphasize on the possibilities of overcoming the situation of backwardness given the empirical evidence of the Finnish and Chinese case studies, as well as learnings for Latin America. The results of the previous chapter on the clash among predominant development pathways in the global stage, as well as the facts of the presidential election in the United States in 2020, outline a possible New Cold War as a process of States rehierarchization after the pandemic crisis.

CHAPTER 2

The Socio–Space–Time Relativity of the State

In Marxist historical materialism, the State is a social construction that results from the division of society into social classes. To guarantee the viability of the social division of capitalist labor, it breaks into the man–nature relationship, placing itself before subjects as embodiment of their community being, formally appearing equal in the political sphere and legitimizing their inequality in the social sphere.[1] Later, Marx and Engels would sketch the principle of Hegemony from the ruling classes toward the subordinate ones as an instrument to maintain the cohesion of the State,[2] also defining the essential objective of the modern State: "... the unfettered development of bourgeois society, the free play of private interests..." (Marx & Engels, 1967, p. 190). Thus, at the base of the capitalist structure made by the division of society into social classes and its conditioning by the social division of labor, the ruling class needs to place its

[1] In Marx's *Critique of Hegel's Philosophy of the State and Law*. He states that: "Through a progress in history, the political classes have been transformed into social classes, so that the different members of the people – as well as the Christians are equal in heaven and unequal on earth – they are equal in the sky of their political world and unequal in the earthly existence of society" (Marx, 1975a, p. 126).

[2] "Only political superstition can still imagine in our day that bourgeois life must be kept in cohesion by the State, when in fact it is the other way around, that it is the State that is maintained in cohesion by bourgeois life" (Marx & Engels, 1967, p. 187).

C. M. Sánchez Ramírez, *Knowledge Capitalism and State Theory*, Palgrave Insights into Apocalypse Economics,
https://doi.org/10.1007/978-3-030-71411-6_2

interest as a general interest through a superstructural construction, with its own and independent form. They introduce it as an "illusory community" that absorbs the representation of the common interest through different stages and phases of development of the mode of production of which it is expression[3] (Marx & Engels, 1970).

These theoretical foundations of the State in Marx enable Marxist thought to address the problems of the State in its socio-political dimension. It means the scientific development of the alienation of labor theory, which conceives the State as a complex superstructure of mediation and social condensation capable of passing between the different historical epochs of the system itself.[4]

Authors like Engels and Lenin advance in the understanding of the double character of consensus and coercion of the State respectively, as fundamental elements in the achievement of its objective: to make appear the maximum expansion of the ruling class as the maximum social expansion. During the unfolding of a new phase of capitalism development in the last quarter of the nineteenth century, Engels states in the introduction to the 1895 edition of *The Class Struggle in France from 1848 to 1850* that a transformation process of domination forms from the dominant classes to the subordinate ones begun in parallel to the bourgeois State. This new forms overcame the role of bourgeois class board of administration of common businesses (Marx & Engels, 1965), as Marx and Engels described the role of the State in the Communist Party Manifesto. This to incorporate a series of non-coercive instruments "as the only way to interest the masses of the people in their plans" (Marx, 1975b, pp. 16–17), such as universal suffrage, the legalization of unions and certain social benefits to the working class.

[3] "The structural characteristics that define the capitalist mode of production (privatization of the community, exploitation, etc.) favor that social subjects are marginalized from the possibility of constructing their social being in a direct, free and conscious way; this can be seen in the fact that the State monopolizes the social project. Separation between the social and the political that can only be overcome by destroying everything that makes society function under the dominance of the economy (the basis of the class struggle and the exteriority that makes the State necessary)" (Juanes, 1982, p. 492).

[4] "Since the State is the form in which the individuals of a ruling class assert their common interests and in which the entire civil society of a time is condensed, it follows that all common institutions have the State as mediator and acquire through it a political form" (Marx & Engels, 1970, p. 72).

In the 1917 Russian Revolution scenario, in a situation of *war of movements* or *permanent Revolution*.[5] contextualized in the building of communism in an industrially underdeveloped economy, Lenin (1978) relativizes Engels' statement about universal suffrage as an instrument of consensual dominance of the bourgeoisie. Resuming Engels' theoretical–conceptual developments in *The Origin of Family, Private Property and State*,[6] Lenin emphasizes that the State is a result of the division of society into social classes at a certain stage of economic development. The existence of the State expresses the irreconcilable character of antagonism and social conflict, becoming an organ of oppression of one class over the other (Lenin, 1978), for which it mainly uses the army, the police and the prison as coercive instruments that legalize and strengthen the power of the dominant groups over the subordinates.

The inclusion in the State of new instruments of consensus described by Engels, that is, the incorporation into the State of non-coercive apparatuses of Hegemony, implied, according to Gramsci, an expansion of the State. This process of expansion from the coercive field emphasized by Lenin to the scope of the State consensus envisioned by Engels required the construction of a set of categories to analyze the class–society, society–State and State–class relations; relationships that serve as a mediation,

[5] The strategy of Trotsky's permanent revolution raised the need for power taking by the subordinate classes in all processes of historical crisis regardless of the lack of conditions for socialism. The historical crisis point developed from Marx's affirmation in the *Prologue to the contribution to the critique of political economy*, states that certain social relations of production in a society do not disappear as long as they can contain the development of the productive forces. At the same time, new social relations of production do not replace the previous ones until the material conditions of their existence materialize, or are in the process of construction or emergence, which occurs within the old society, within the old social relations of production. Although there is a historical change (the transition from one mode of production to another: from the primitive community to slavery, from slavery to feudalism, from feudalism to capitalism), it is not automatic (Portanteiro, 1977).

[6] "Thus, the State is in no way a power imposed from outside on society; nor is it 'the reality of the moral idea', nor 'the image and reality of reason', as Hegel claims. Rather, it is a product of society when it reaches a certain stage of development: it is the confession that that society has entangled in an irreparable contradiction with itself and is divided by irreconcilable antagonisms, which it is powerless to conjure. But in order that these antagonisms, these classes with competing economic interests, do not devour themselves and do not consume society in a sterile struggle, it is necessary a power apparently above society and called to cushion the shock, to keep them within the limits of 'order'. And that power, born from society, but which rises above it and divorces it more and more, is the State" (Engels, 1989, pp. 141–142).

hinge and fulcrum between the economic structure and the socio-spatial and institutional superstructure. To do this, Gramsci proposes a series of theoretical and operational lenses around the concept of Hegemony that concerns the Marxist theory of the State. Therefore, it is necessary to analyze the socio-economic and techno-economic relations that intervene between the main groups of the dominant classes and the classes subject to their sphere of influence (Buci-Glucksmann, 1979).

Thus, situated in the process of structural transition from mercantilism to capitalism centered on the great monopolies, the Gramscian challenge is to understand the superstructural transformation of the State. He names restricted State or political society to the period of domination based on the coercion of the ruling classes. This stage begins prior to the revolutions of 1848, when capitalism emerged under the absolutist State inherited from feudalism, to later consider the construction of a superstructure based on coercion, functional to structural changes in the social relations of capitalist production. Therefore, the State is the condensation of political relations of the society or area where social coercion is concentrated. There is the preponderance of a set of institutions with a coercive nature such as the army, the police, the courts or the judicial system. It transits to another type of State with new forms of legitimation, which takes place in the last quarter of the nineteenth century, particularly in Germany,[7] which had positioned itself as a new axis of economic–political development, after the war with France and the defeat of the Paris Commune in 1871.

In this process, the political form of the modern State develops, characterized by the expansion and active role of a new civil society, which includes and transcends parliamentary and bureaucratic mediations that legitimize the State through the vote, incorporating the masses and the power and interest groups located in companies, unions and civil associations. This forces a shift in the orientation of the political dispute of the lower classes. It means the replacement of the old strategy of *permanent Revolution*, characterized by a continuous *war of movements*—the

[7] Mainly as a consequence of popular struggles, the State "ceases to be a traditional liberal to become a new mass democracy, open to a political struggle based on the broad recognition of rights and duties of social organizations such as unions, parties, ex-combatants, organs of public opinion and with new bureaucratic mediations of education, police, and social security open to regulation and citizen participation, both urban and rural" (Oliver, 2013, pp. 61–62).

spontaneous mobilization of unconscious masses led by conscious minorities—for *civil Hegemony or war of positions*[8]—participation and struggle of an organized and conscious society in the different spheres of the State and civil society—(Oliver, 2013).

This increase in political–social rights as a projection of structural changes in a new phase of development implied the expansion of new forms of relationship between civil society and political society based on consensus.[9] This corresponds to an organic transformation of the State in an expanded or full State, which transcends the coercive scope of the ruling elites[10] and extends their hegemonic capacity by attracting to their sphere of influence the activity of organizations, institutions and actors of civil society from the exercise of consensus. Therefore, the concept of full State[11] encompasses both dimensions of the State, as a political society and as a civil society "… because it should be noted that in the general notion of State, there are elements that must be brought back to the notion of civil society (in this sense, it could be said, that State = political society + civil society, that is, Hegemony armored by coercion)" (Gramsci, 1981, TIII, p. 76). It is the State as a condensation of political relations, it is no longer only the sphere where coercion is concentrated, but it is also the sphere of the exercise of consensus.

The full State concept represents an advance to understand the achievement of the political objective of the State to create favorable conditions for the maximum expansion of the ruling class and present it as a

[8] The transition from the strategy of permanent revolution to the strategy of civil Hegemony also implies that, before considering the seizure of power and being dominant, the subaltern classes must be leaders. Civil Hegemony is an instrument that articulates consensus capacity with coercion capacity, to build a new social order. From a historical crisis as a starting point, and following a strategy of obtaining hegemonic positions in civil society, subaltern groups gradually take the reproduction of social management in their hands, building the alternative project that will be promoted later with the seizure of political power.

[9] Capacity of consensus implies leadership capacity, capacity of a class or social group to convince most of society about the justice of its historical purposes.

[10] Coercion is the ability to compel certain social groups to take as their own the historical objectives of the class that exercises Hegemony.

[11] "The conception of the full State presupposes that all the means of intellectual and moral direction of a class over society are taken into account, the way in which it can achieve its Hegemony, even when it is the price of compromise balances tending to safeguard its own political power, particularly threatened in periods of crisis" (Buci-Glucksmann, 1979, p. 123).

universal expansion (Gramsci, 1980, 1996, 2009; Buci-Glucksmann, 1979). Based on the set of practical and theoretical activities with which the ruling class not only justifies and maintains its dominance (field corresponding to political society), it manages to obtain the active consensus of the governed (corresponding to civil society) (Gramsci, 1980, 1981, 1996, 2009; Buci-Glucksmann, 1979). The ruling classes carry out their Hegemony over the subalterns that way.

Among the tasks to create favorable conditions to the maximum expansion of the dominant group is the extension of the instruments of the State to fulfill its economic function of adapting the lower classes to the economic production apparatus (Buci-Glucksmann, 1979). This marks the importance of establishing an additional conceptual element that organically links the economic structure with the superstructural complex, taking into account that every social group "is born in the original terrain of an essential function in the world of economic production" (Sacristán, 2013). Therefore, Gramsci synthesizes the dilemma of organically linking the structural economic framework with class–society–State relations in the concept of Historic Bloc.

The starting point for the Gramscian Historic Bloc analysis is a Marx statement in the *Prologue to the contribution to the critique of political economy* (Portanteiro, 1977). "A social formation never perishes until all the productive forces have been developed to which is amply sufficient, and new and superior relations of production never take their place before their conditions of existence have not been incubated within the old society itself. Hence, humanity always set itself only tasks that it can solve, considering it more deeply, we will always find that the task itself only arises when the material conditions for its resolution already exist or, at least, are in the process of becoming" (Marx, 1982, p. 67); that Gramsci sets as the structural conditions for the evolution of the Historic Bloc within the limits of the development of the economic structure (crisis situation), based on the praxis of social groups in the superstructural field (Gramsci, 1981).

In the Historic Bloc, the set of political, ideological and cultural praxis must be functional to the structure, that is, organize and direct the set of social groups in accordance with socio-economic conditions (Portelli, 1977). Although the Historic Bloc presupposes a ruling class that exercises its Hegemony over a set of diverse social strata, the concept goes beyond a simple class alliance, since it in turn implies the complex development of superstructures, the realization of a full State (Buci-Glucksmann, 1979). The set of superstructures encompass the ideology and politics of the different social groups, from which they are aware of the structural contradictions, reflected in the notion of the Historic Bloc where the economics determines the politics in what concerns the State sphere.

Nevertheless, the achievement of the objective of full State unity requires a Passive Revolution[12] process in which the ruling classes obtain the passive or active consensus of the subordinate ones and eliminate the antagonistic social forces (Buci-Glucksmann, 1979). This means the incorporation of the historical interests and objectives of the subordinate classes, foreign to the ruling classes and even contrary to them, thus achieving a consensus based on a future project that represents a real possibility of development for the lower classes.[13]

The concepts of full State and Historic Bloc, which turn around the concept of Hegemony, have the national scale as their main reference. However, their international projection is a function of the convening capacity of a certain State to make its development modality or pathway, a world reference for the aspirations of progress of other States, in order to find a place for their aspirations for progress without neglecting their national specificities. In function of this convening capacity, the State representing the progressive forces of history, becomes a hegemonic power, leader and guide of a system of alliances and agreements of greater or less extension (Gramsci, 1981), forming an International System of States Hegemony or World Order.

Although achieving this international convening capacity is crucial in the hegemonic aspirations of a great power, there are other elements derived from the strength and consolidation of this power's own

[12] Gramsci explains the Passive Revolution or Restoration Revolution as "the needs of the 'thesis' to develop fully, to the point of incorporating a part of the antithesis itself, so as not to be 'overcome', that is, in the dialectical opposition only the thesis, in fact, developed all its possibilities of struggle until winning over those who claim to be representatives of the antithesis" (Gramsci, 1981, TV, p. 188).

[13] Gramsci distinguishes a specificity in the processes of Passive Revolution, starting from the "fact that a State substitutes local social groups to lead a renewal struggle. It is one of the cases in which the function of "dominance" and not of "leadership" occurs in these groups: dictatorship without Hegemony" (Gramsci, 1981, TV, p. 233).

economic structure that allow the deployment of its "national solution" on a global scale. Gramsci expresses these elements in terms of determining a hierarchy of power between States:

> Elements to calculate the hierarchy of power between States:
>
> 1] territory extension, 2] economic force, 3] military force.
>
> The way in which being a great power is manifested is given by the possibility of giving State activity an autonomous direction, whose influence and repercussion must be suffered by other States: the great power is the hegemonic power, leader and guide of a system of alliances and of agreements of greater or lesser extension. Military strength summarizes the value of the territorial extension (with an adequate population, naturally) and of the economic potential. At the territorial moment, the geographical position must be specifically considered. In economic strength, industrial and agricultural capacity (productive forces) must be distinguished from financial capacity. An "imponderable" element is the "ideological" position that a country occupies in the world at any given moment, as to considered a representative of the progressive forces of history (example of France during the Revolution of 1789 and the Napoleonic period).
>
> These elements are calculated in the perspective of a war. Having all the elements that, within the limits of the foreseeable, give assurance of victory, means having a potential for diplomatic pressure of great power, that is, it means obtaining a part of the results of a victorious war without the need to fight. (Gramsci, 1999, volume V, notebook 13, p. 47)

The transition from the political sphere of the State discussed above to its economic sphere driven by a critical perspective requires getting over neoclassical growth theory as an equilibrium process and the implementation of Keynesianism without taking into account national specificities. Therefore, theoretical developments discussed below downplay the importance of capital accumulation as a prerequisite for overcoming economic backwardness and highlight the economic action of the State due to its historical and strategic capacity in promoting growth and economic development from a situation of economic underdevelopment.

Gerschenkron (1968) focused on the first experiences of overcoming economic backwardness in European countries during the second half of the nineteenth century and before WWI. The starting discussion point is what he calls the "hidden half" in Marx's prologue of *Das Kapital*: "The industrially more developed countries put to the less progressive countries the mirror of their own future" (Marx, 2001, p. XIV). Because backwardness implies the existence of other advanced countries, this circumstance leads to a pathway of a backward country that differs in character and pace from that followed by the advanced country, derived from the economic strategies applied in the first, which the second did not need to carry out. Furthermore, Gerschenkron discusses the universal meaning of the initial conditions or prerequisites for the industrial development of a backward country, particularly the availability of capital or "primitive accumulation" that Marx points out in *Das Kapital*.

> It is true that during the period between the middle and the end of the last century, Germany followed the pathway that England had previously taken. Nevertheless, we should not completely accept the aforementioned generalization, since we risk that the half-truth that it contains, hides the other half; that is, due to the mere fact of its backwardness, the development of a backward country may differ fundamentally, in many important aspects, from that followed by an advanced country. (Gerschenkron, 1968, pp. 16–17)

Gerschenkron states that it is possible to distinguish the specificity of backwardness, that is, the possibility of classifying countries according to the degree of backwardness in which they are, based on their production levels, technological progress, the educational level of its population and business organization, as well as grouping those with a similar degree of development. Therefore he distinguishes Germany, Austria, Italy, Switzerland and France national pathways as a first group of backward experiences that received a powerful positive impulse from industrial banking, serving as a source of finance of the long-term investment needs of those economies. This unlike the industrialization process in England[14] as an advanced country of the time, which was carried out without a substantial use of banking to finance long-term investments.

In contrast to this first set of backward countries is the Russian experience, which during the nineties of the nineteenth century presented the same basic elements of backwardness as Germany in the fifties of the same

[14] "There is no doubt that factory building in England benefited considerably from the existence of many sources of private wealth. Precisely one of the characteristics of the development of this country is the fact that prior to it there was considerable progress that made individuals feel a great desire to invest for industrial purposes" (Gerschenkron, 1968, p. 53).

century. However, Russia had extraordinary quantitative differences than Germany, mainly because the shortage of capital was so great that banking systems were unable to finance large-scale industrial development. Thus, it was the State the most important foster of economic progress, which acquired a jerky, fast or slow character as required by military needs.

> In order to obtain the capital that industrialization required, the operation of the State machine was necessary, which, with its obligatory power, and through its tax policy, managed to divert income from consumption to investment. (Gerschenkron, 1968, p. 29)

The historical study carried out by Gerschenkron (1968) points out the role of the Russian State in overcoming backwardness, where he affirms that a government like that "can only stay in power if it manages to make people to believe that it is performing an important social function that in its absence could not be carried out" (p. 37). This highlights the general Marxist vision of the political dimension of the State as a superstructural construction that absorbs the representation of the common interest and the Gramscian specificity in which in backward countries prevail a restricted State or political society as a condensation sphere of coercion. Therefore, the use of State instruments to fulfill its economic function of creating the necessary conditions for production and accumulation becomes a strategic objective of its economic dimension.

To achieve this objective, the State can deploy a set of tools in the economic sphere, related to the degree of backwardness of the country. An initial action made possible by the "advantage of backwardness" is the absorption by the backward country of a certain baggage of technological innovations that the advanced country did not have at its disposal in its own industrialization process. This is the propensity of a backward country to focus on productive areas where technological progress is more recent, which represent sources of technical assistance such as capital goods and specialized labor; being more important to concentrate in the development of those industrial branches in which more recent and faster technological advances have been registered.

In the case of the German economic development until WWI, Gerschenkron points out that the activities in which the attention of German banks concentrated were those corresponding to heavy industry, made up of mines of coal, steel industry, general electrical machinery production and heavy chemical production, while relegated the activities of the textile, leather and food products industry. Similarly, the Russian State in the nineties of the nineteenth century did not show interest in light industry, but based on a strong restricted State action,[15] focused entirely on large-scale companies, whose creation it had favored through the production of basic industrial materials and machinery.

An additional lever of industrialization in the hands of the State is the deployment of physical infrastructure, as a general condition for reproduction and accumulation, and the impulse of external economies associated with it from the development of national industries that provide inputs and services in preferred conditions. This strategy led to a great industrial boom in Russia during the second half of the eighties of the nineteenth century, when the State construction of railways had a strong expansion, promoting in turn a rapid industrialization by requesting the supplies needed to national producers and implementing a policy of high prices, subsidies and credits to new industrial companies.

Gerschenkron argues that a characteristic of backwardness is that development does not necessarily occur in a "classical" way. Proof of this is that a period of rapid industrialization does not necessarily has as "prerequisite" a long period of capital accumulation. According to his economic–historical analysis, in the most backward countries of the European continent, the size of the availability of capital reached by previous accumulations, and even the investment capacity and commitment to the industrialization process of the industrial bourgeoisie were insufficient for the needs and demands of capital in a situation of late industrialization. Under this scenario presents three "possible types of substitution" for the absent factor of capital accumulation in the industrialization process under backward conditions. The first was the German banking system and its policy of granting loans (development bank) as the most representative example. The second was the strategic role of the budgetary policies of the Russian State. In addition, the third was the import of foreign capital aimed at productive investments, as a way of reducing the importance that the national wealth created previously may have.

[15] The Russian State carried out the task of adapting the subaltern classes to the economic apparatus of production, imposing heavy workloads on the generations whose life span coincided with the stages of intense development, even subjecting them to various measures of oppression, to prevent them from escaping through the southern and southeastern border regions (Gerschenkron, 1968, pp. 26–27).

An additional characteristic of the backwardness of the countries is that the development process is not necessarily linear, but can acquire a spasmodic character depending on the native elements of a specific country: fast or slow as required by stages and degree of backwardness. In a country located in a deep position of underdevelopment like Russia, the State managed to reduce this condition, sponsoring the process of industrial development, substituting the capital that industrialization required, through a tax policy that managed to divert consumer income to investment. Gradually, as the development gap closed, the St. Petersburg-based deposit banks replaced those of Moscow and operated according to the principles of German banking in the field of industrial investment, becoming instruments for the organization and development of the economy. Finally, the reorganization of the tax system in the country to finance industrialization as well as a monetary policy to stabilize the currency and the introduction of the gold standard encouraged foreign participation in the development of Russian industry. This opened the possibility of continuing the productive investment process without the need to decrease the current consumption rate, which is more difficult to achieve through the credit policies of banks or government spending financing practices through taxes.

In addition to describe the previous economic strategy by the State to overcome the situation of backwardness, Gerschenkron also outlines the need to deepen the training and qualification of the workforce in order to enhance their physical (and cognitive) strength, thus emphasizes that the general prospects for industrialization of an underdeveloped country are generally based on the lower relative price that variable capital usually has with respect to constant capital and in the consequent difficulty in substituting abundant labor for scarce constant capital.

Coinciding with Gerschenkron, Hirschman (1964) also rejected the idea of the necessary overcoming of backwardness from a classical process of economic development. In controversy with neoclassical economics and its balanced growth thought, and even against post-WWII prevailing Keynesianism, Hirschman developed a set of strategies for economic development with special emphasis to Latin America economies. Thus, and again in a similar way to that proposed by Gerschenkron, he qualifies as little useful the concept of initial capital stock as a "prerequisite" for growth and economic development, proposing as a "type of possible substitution" the impulse of the State to maintain and promote "tensions, disproportions and imbalances" in the development process. This "unbalancing and inducing" function of the State in a situation of backwardness implies increasing its capacity to make new investment decisions, taking advantage of the creation of external economies and their complementary effects, particularly in situations of scarcity, such as those found in the underdeveloped countries.

For Hirschman, the "advantage of backwardness" in an underdeveloped country is the possibility of the State to expand the sphere of action of its induced investment decisions, making economic growth depend on the continuous emergence of profitable opportunities, that is, creating imbalances that induce constructive action. This "unbalanced growth"—in contrast to the idea of neoclassical "balanced growth" where all activities expand evenly—means inducing a set of uneven advances in an industrial sector to trigger development in others in their attempt to reach and surpass the former.

> Therefore, the sequence that "takes us away from equilibrium" is precisely the ideal pattern of development: each step in the sequence is induced by a previous imbalance and, in turn, creates a new imbalance that requires an additional step. This is achieved because the expansion of industry A produces external economies for A, but which B can be appropriated, while the consequent expansion of B brings with it external economies for B, but subsequently internal economies for A (or in this case for C), etc. etc. At every step, an industry takes advantage of external economies created by previous expansion and, at the same time, creates new external economies that other producers can exploit. (Hirschman, 1964, p. 74)

This way, in achieving the objective of economic development in a backward situation, non-market forces—such as the State—are not necessarily "less automatic" than market forces, particularly in view of the need to elaborate a development strategy. In the perspective of a process of unbalanced growth, when difficulties do not overcome immediately with the resources available internally, the State can incorporate capital investment from abroad, in order to boost those sectors of greater potential of the economy for rapid growth (Hirschman, 1964).

To complete this analytical theoretical journey on the role of the State in economic development, it is important to take into account the study on the relatively recent experiences of the East Asian nations and its economic take-off, particularly the cases of South Korea and Taiwan. From the institutionalist thought, Evans (2007) argues that these countries achieved a successful insertion into contemporary capitalism through a developmental State, understood as an institutional innovation that reconfigures relations between the State, economy and civil society. Based on Marx (the State as a representative of "the social"), Gerschenkron (the State as a possible substitute for original accumulation), and Hirschman (the State inducing an unbalanced growth), Evans considers as institutional innovation of the State, the continuous, organized and controlled interventionism. This allowed England its opening toward the free market, as well as the rise of the "late development countries" such as Germany and Russia, which depended on the State for the construction of markets and the promotion of investment banking.

In the case of East Asian developmental states, their rise into the world economic hierarchy presented important connections between global markets, the State and civil society through an "embedded autonomy." This is the capacity of the State to achieve relative autonomy from the dominant groups and simultaneously maintain ties with them, based on the deployment of infrastructure, granting of subsidies and protection against external competition, in exchange for the built of an industrial capacity internationally competitive. The emphasis on State action in recent Asian developmental nations contrasts with the dominant global ideology about the convenience of an absent or "overshadowed" State, related to a supposed crisis of its management capacity, caused by the intense dynamics of economic relations on the supranational scale.

The economic relations in the global stage that limit the national scope are expressed in a greater increase in exports and imports compared to local and national transactions, the growth of the exports proportion in relation to GDP and the increased foreign direct investment compared to trade. Furthermore, the integration of global production chains on a multiplicity of territorial scales and a globally organized financial system. In contrast to the discursive tendency of the "evaporation" of the State, Evans[16] suggests that the vulnerability of a country to external shocks caused by greater trade openness is balanced with a deepen role of the

[16] Evans (2007) considers analyzes carried out by Garret, Kitschell, Lange Marks and Stephens, who show that the configuration of public institutions continues to modify the impact of globalization. He warns that, using data from the eighties and nineties of the twentieth century, Rodrik finds a strong correlation in OECD countries between public spending as a percentage of GDP and their openness to trade, concluding that countries that are more open trade, have larger State administrations. This trend is repeated

State. This expressed in an increase in public spending and administration so that an active role of the State in the economic sphere is a comparative and competitive advantage for a country in the global arena.

Under this approach, the successful insertion of the East Asian developmental nations into contemporary capitalism would be the result of intense connections between the State, the economy and civil society. This triangular relationship is a dynamic institutional innovation that corresponds to the continuous evolution of the structural economic elements of the capitalist system and that poses new challenges in the political and institutional spheres, both on the national and global scales. To overcome this challenge, Evans proposes to transcend the sterile debate between the market and the State in the absence of civil society, and to advance to the recognition of the State and the economy as reciprocally constitutive spheres that require the establishment of institutional structures that limit or expand markets, but built from the interaction between State and civil society.

Evans understands civil society as the relationship between different social groups—such as workers, businesspersons and other interest groups—that have a common cultural background and share institutional and organizational forms that make economic action possible. There is a dialectical relationship between civil society and State institutions, where the latter structure the former, but civil society shapes State action too. In this way, development would not be an isolated product from the capacity of the markets, but rather a function of its connection with civil society and the institutional structures of the State.

In the case of backward countries, an institutional innovation under the triangular scheme between the State, the economy and civil society is the one proposed by Evans as a "renewed embedded liberalism,"[17] which

when expanding the analysis to more than one hundred countries, most of them developing, in which he finds "a surprising positive correlation between the size of the state administration and its openness to trade" (p. 104).

[17] By embedded liberalism Evans refers to developed countries after WWII when the solution to social conflict provided by Fordism—Keynesianism was the recognition of class conflict and the organization of social classes in large corporations of businessmen, workers, farmers, day laborers, etc., who negotiate the distribution of the economic surplus as a way to achieve growth based on domestic demand. As a triumphant power in the war conflict and together with the emerging international institutional framework (World Bank and the International Monetary Fund), the United States promotes Fordism—Keynesianism through the Marshall Plan, as a model to be followed by European countries

guarantees the conditions of reproduction and accumulation of capital and keeps civil society isolated from its costs through increases in real wages and local investments. A renewed embedded liberalism requires the establishment of relationships of mutual empowerment or synergy between the institutions of the State and an organized civil society, leading to an increase in the management and action capacity of the State based on new structures for governance and institutional frameworks. These new economic structures should incubate predictable economic decisions for national and international investment flows, ensuring the protection of their benefits, especially those that come from intangible assets, as well as put in place effective instruments to achieve collective goals around the development and coproduction of services, preventing society from providing more resources mainly in times of scarcity.

Evans emphasizes the need to consider the spatial dimension of social relations, particularly at the supranational scale, where it is also necessary to update the institutional innovation of the State in order to contain and reverse the shaping of the national geography of the State by the global capitalism geography. Even in supranational scope where globalized financial capitalism predominates, it depends on the economic action of the State—at the national scale—to defend the value of the currencies in which its main assets are located. Furthermore, the State should establish regulatory frameworks (effectively implemented) for trade and to assure profit rates derived from the use of physical or intangible private property. However, the open access markets policy must be embedded to effective social protection that also depends on the triangular relationship between the State, the market and civil society, in which the latter finds new organizational forms on the global scale that allow it to influence State actions in its relationship with international markets.

Thus, Evans' institutionalist approach on the economic role of the State corresponds to Gramsci's full State concept. This results in similar approaches from economics and politics developed under different theoretical assumptions where the spatial dimension of the State does not appear fully integrated, requiring in-depth discussion as follows.

Even though in the classic works of Marx, Engels and Lenin, there are elements on the expansive territorial trend of capitalism, which provide

in the reconstruction process. By controlling exchange rates, the United States inhibited trade wars and competitive devaluations, ensuring that countries based their growth process on domestic demand following American—Fordist model.

the first trace for the study and spatial analysis of the capitalist system, those were underdeveloped in subsequent theoretical approaches. Among the reasons for the poor initial development of the space analysis and its appreciation as a container or an external reflection of the social relations dynamics, Soja (1989) argues the delay in the translation of *The Grundrisse* until after WWII. This Marx's work contains the greatest number of references to geographical analysis than any of his other works, including the expansive geographical tendency of capitalism, which would later be expressed in the third volume (and the projected later) of *Das Kapital*. Based on the historical and geographical analysis of the world market, colonialism, international trade and the role of the State, Marx approaches to the uneven geographical development of production, regions and countries.

A second element is the one presented by Lefebvre (2013) in relation to Marxist analysis, not only as the materialist critique of Hegelian idealism, but also as the reluctance to conceive the space as a socio-historical product. This contrasts to the Hegelian thought of subordinating time to space, the former being a historical process shaped by a territorial "spirit": the State. Finally, the conditions of exploitation in the first stages of capitalism development privileged the production of the space from the molding forces of the market and the State, encapsulated in a temporary arrangement centered on the rate of exploitation as a fundamental measure of socially necessary work time. This led to the fact that in the absolute surplus value extraction the social organization of time appeared more important than the social organization of space.

Contrasting the space understanding that prevailed until the second half of the twentieth century, confining it as a simple cultural expression in the field of the superstructure, Lefebvre discusses the need to articulate the structural economic base with the socio-spatial plot. He states that space and the political organization of space are a result of social relations, but the latter are also a product of the former, establishing dynamic, dialectical and interdependent socio-spatial relations. Therefore, the social relations of production, in parallel, produce spaces and take place in them. In accordance with Lefebvre, Mandel (1976) also identified the problem of space on its regional and international scales, stating that uneven development between regions and countries is an essential result of the capitalist system, in the same way as the exploitation of labor by capital, thus placing uneven geographical development as a crucial factor for the accumulation process and a determinant for the reproduction of the capitalist system.

Regarding the problem of space in its relationship with capitalism and the State, Gramsci's early approach is important. He does not address the problem explicitly, but his work introduces theoretical embryos showing evidence of the spatial relationships included in the social formation and its different territorial scales. Based on his analysis of the urban and regional aspects and the alliances between the subaltern classes belonging to both scales, the Gramscian contribution to the spatial dimension of the State focuses on the emphasis placed on the territorial imposition of the social division of labor. In a similar way to his contribution to the political dimension of the State, on its transit from its restricted sense to its broad sense, the concept of Hegemony becomes central in its spatial dimension. While its realization through a social structure implies a territoriality, it implicitly reflects the understanding of a Gramscian socio-spatial dialectic, through which the principle of Hegemony resizes spatially.

This socio-spatial dialectic relates to the exploitation of the subaltern classes in their places of residence and the spatial differentiation between those as spaces of production and spaces of reproduction and consumption. From this perspective, concerning to the full State as the set of ruling classes practices to maintain their rule and Historic Bloc as the agreements between social classes around a historical project, its spatial dimension appears clearly by emphasizing the spheres where the realization of Hegemony by the ruling classes toward the subaltern ones takes place. This "geographic imposition of labor" proposed by Gramsci is explained by Lefebvre (2013) as the production of space by the State. Based on the requirement of ordered spaces according to the specific requirements of the institutions that make up the State, it imposes in the space its capitalist rationality.

The incessant spatial action of the State has a hegemonic purpose by making appear the chaotic spaces produced by capitalism homogeneous to the whole society. The ruling class praxis to justify its dominance, which Gramsci explains as a full State, acquires its spatial dimension when the State imposes and maintains a hierarchical system of scales, functions and institutions. This guarantees the capital conditions of accumulation and reproduction carried out in space, such as the reproduction of labor force, the means of production and the relations of production. In the face of the expansive territorial tendency of capitalism, the State organizes the space in order to break the tensions inherent to the historic social conflict between capital and labor, hierarchizing the geographical scales based on power relations and assuming control of the entire territorial system.

Thus, in developed countries where Historic Blocs tend to have stronger hegemonic function, meaning a civil society with a relatively higher degree of development than political society corresponding to a full State, the space produced by the State to guarantee the general conditions of reproduction of capital tends to be a homogeneous, fractured and hierarchical space.

> The space produced by the State is homogeneous, which implies a property of exchange in space and time, taking the form of an identical and repetitive process. It is fractured for use in a set of activities, such as work and recreation, which take place in different places; and hierarchical by conforming unequal spatial arrangements in relation to the center, from the centers of power to the impoverished but equally state – controlled peripheries. (Lefebvre, 2003, p. 94)

The historical analysis carried out by Lefebvre on the production of space by the State agrees with Gramsci in pointing out the changes that took place in the last quarter of the nineteenth century in Western Europe. It means the transit of the State toward the use of new forms to legitimate the socio-political contradiction through consensus, extending State regulatory controls over the entire spectrum of places, sites, regions and scales within national borders. It is during this period and the first years of the following century that the European States began to channel a set of investment resources aimed at the construction of physical infrastructure through their territories, including ports, canals, bridges, tunnels, railways, housing, public services and communication networks. The massive State investment in infrastructure to guarantee the conditions of accumulation, reproduction and circulation of capital produced new patterns of uneven geographical development within national territories, as well as socio-spatial polarization of the capital–labor conflict, due to systematic action of the State that prioritized public and private investment of some territorial scales over others.

Subsequently, the postwar welfare State developed and articulated through its institutional apparatus deployed at different scalar levels, a set of compensatory actions designed to homogenize the industrial, population and investment deployment and infrastructure investment throughout the territory. It alleviates the effects of the spatial pattern of uneven development inherited from the past, establishing minimum standards of social welfare and public services throughout the national territory. However, from the seventies of the last century the State eroded the promotion of scales homogenization projects within the national space, in the wake of a reorientation of financial resources to strengthen the cities infrastructure, more competitive metropolitan regions and technology centers in the global arena. To carry out these tasks, specific State institutional arrangements adapted to the specific socio-economic conditions of the geographic scales involved.

This reterritorialization, rehierarchization of scales and the establishment of specific spatial forms in which the States focuses its socio-economic policy is one of the key transformations of the State spatiality in contemporary capitalism. It characterizes by the erosion of its capacity for scalar homogenization of its institutional arrangement and the emergence of divergent levels in the provision of public services throughout the national territories. Jessop describes this process as follows:

> There is no new privileged scale, which other levels organize around in order to guarantee a coherent structure within and across scales. Instead, there is a continuous struggle over which scale should become the main one and how the other scales should articulate around it, and this reflects in a more complex nesting and interweaving of different scales as they are re – articulated. (Jessop, 2002, p. 179)

Under these previous historic–theoretical substrates,[18] Brenner (2004) develops a theoretical framework that allows addressing the production of spaces by the actions of the capitalist State as a process. Brenner agrees with Lefebvre in the need to overcome the fetishized vision of space, which conceives it exclusively in Cartesian terms as a surface where economic activity takes place, to understand it simultaneously as a precondition, a means and a result of capitalist social relations in continuous change. Brenner argues that the State does not produce spaces simply

[18]Within the historical analysis, it is important to consider that the emergence of the nation State is located in the sixteenth century, given the need of the rising bourgeoisie to consolidate territorial spaces that would become markets for their new products. This original process brings together the particles of territory derived from the previous feudal system, and represents the beginning of a continuous process of spatial transformation of the State that has taken various forms over time throughout the different phases of capitalism development.

filled as if they were pre-established territorial containers, but produces and actively transforms them through the dense set of the socio-spatial interaction with the institutional apparatus of the State in the scope of many geographic scales. To do this, he distinguishes two moments of State spatiality: in a restricted sense and in an integral sense.

The spatiality of the State in a restricted sense refers to the distinctive form of the spatial organization of the State as territorially deployed, self-contained and internally differentiated in institutional apparatus. This internal territorial differentiation implies the establishment of specific institutional forms based on different geographic scales (urban, rural and border areas), which cover certain administrative arrangements. These scalar divisions of regulation can provide the State with a framework of action that is relatively stable during a certain period and modified according to the social conflict, reorganizing the institutional structure and the functions of the administrative units of the scales involved.

On the other hand, the spatiality of the State in an integral sense refers to the territorial specificity in which the institutional apparatus of the State is oriented, in order to regulate social relations and influence the localities in which these relations take place. This is the continuous geographic intervention of the State in the socio-economic processes within a determined territorial scale. Based on this spatial action of the State in space, its institutional apparatus tries to guarantee the conditions of accumulation and reproduction of capital, territorially strengthening specific localities in order to accelerate the circulation of capital, reproduce the workforce and address specific socio-economic problems in order to maintain territorial cohesion around the geographic centers of economic activity.

This State action produces unequal spatial effects due to the differentiated intervention of the State in territorial scales under specific conditions, so the uneven geographical development derived from the unequal action of the State represents an important characteristic of the spatiality of the State in an integral sense. Both aspects of the spatiality of the State, in a restricted and integral sense, intertwine and produce specific historical formations of State spatiality, in which each form of State produces a specific form of space and capitalist administration of it, as well as socio-spatial relations.

From that theoretical development, Brenner inspires himself by Jessop's concept of "strategic selectivity" in order to advance in the construction of an analytical apparatus of greater specificity that facilitates the study of the configuration of the spatiality of the capitalist

State. According to Jessop, an accumulation strategy is established when a certain model of economic growth or development pathway is linked to a State institutional framework with enough capacity to carry it out. In this way, strategic selectivity aims to the set of political strategies that shape the device of institutional structures of the State and its forms of socio-economic intervention, which result from privileging the particular interests of certain groups and social agents over the rest of social fractions. This is what Gramsci states as the creation of favorable conditions for the maximum expansion of the ruling class to present it as universal expansion.

In this strategic selectivity of the State, Jessop carries out an analytical distinction in two moments: the first of them related to those strategies oriented toward the institutional structure of the State or State projects and the second related to the strategies implemented in order to carry out the hegemonic exercise within civil society or State strategies. State projects aim to provide State institutions with a certain homogeneity in their operation, operational coordination and organizational coherence, having an impact on the strategic selectivity of the State to the extent that certain social groups predominate in the dynamic institutional structure of government power. State strategies point toward the specific configuration of State institutions in order to carry out certain forms of socio-economic intervention, and their influence on the strategic selectivity of the State is a function of the hegemonic capacity of a social sector to influence the dynamic role of the State as guarantor of the conditions for the realization of capital.

Beyond placing it as a pre-established characteristic of the State, Jessop's conception of State's strategic selectivity puts it as the result of dialectic social relations. From this perspective, social conflict dynamically shapes the institutional structure of the State, as well as the State forms of economic intervention and accumulation strategies in order to guarantee the hegemonic exercise by the ruling classes. Hence, Brenner argues that the State endows with a spatial dimension, which in turn has a certain spatial selectivity referred to the processes of spatial articulation and predominance, from which the State implements a set of institutional policies differentiated in the territorial space in order to influence certain scales[19] and geographical areas.

[19] Because Brenner develops his conceptual theoretical framework on the spatiality of the State from the State theory elaborated by Jessop, it is important to mention that on

Analogously to the strategic selectivity of the State articulated from State projects and strategies, through the spatial selectivity of the State, it is possible to distinguish State spatial projects and strategies. State space projects correspond to the spatiality of the State in a restricted sense and its objective is to articulate the institutional action of the State between multiple and different territorial scales, configuring a regulated, partitioned, functional, coordinated and organized geography based on the internal division of the State institutional apparatus at the subnational, regional, metropolitan and local scales. State spatial strategies are the expression of the spatiality of the State in an integral sense and deployed in order to influence the geography of industrial development, investment in infrastructure and the socio-political contradiction, based on the active territorial intervention of the institutional apparatus of the State.

This spatial action of the State, which shapes the geography of capitalist accumulation, requires a set of State capacities that make possible the spatial intervention of the State to carry out a spatial structural coherence that guarantees the conditions of territorial reproduction of the capitalist system in the national, regional and local scales. This happens through several State instruments such as industrial, economic, infrastructure, planning, housing and labor development policies. The spatial selectivity derived from the spatial projects and strategies of the State is a function of political–spatial praxis over an economic structure that expresses within the Historic Bloc, allowing prioritize, subordinate or marginalize certain territorial scales.

This results in an uneven geographical development derived from the tendency to different geographical State actions during successive phases of development of the capitalist system. Therefore, State spatiality is uneven and discontinuous in time and is a process of polymorphic stratification in which State spatial projects and strategies are historically superimposed, turning spatiality into a presupposition, medium and product of geographical conditions inherited from the past. Thus, a State

the concept of "scale", Jessop (2002) takes up the approach of Swyngedouw. He defines it as "the space and the moment, discursively and materially, where the socio–spatial relations of power are disputed and agreements are negotiated and regulated. Therefore, scale is the result and outcome of the social dispute for power and control ... [Consequently] the theoretical and political priority... never resides in a particular geographic scale, but rather *in the process* through which particular scales get to be re – constituted" (p. 178).

spatial selectivity emerges from the social conflict enclosed by the State, shaping specific historical forms of State spatiality that intertwine in time.

The above discussion takes a step forward in the formulation of a State theory relative to its space–time dimensions, in order to elaborate the political foundation of the State to undertake an economic and spatial development pathway from a situation of backwardness in a certain stage of capitalism development or phase of development. The political principle of the State of an underdeveloped nation takes place in the absence of leadership of its ruling classes, being necessary a process of Gramscian Passive Revolution where the State substitutes local social groups in order to lead a renewal struggle.

On the one hand, ruling classes of developed countries carry out Hegemony within Historic Bloc achieving an active consensus of subordinate groups around a project of future based on the economic structure of a historical epoch, paving the way to a full State that ensures favorable conditions for the maximum expansion of dominant classes and presents it as a universal expansion. On the other hand, lack of leadership of ruling classes in underdeveloped countries takes to the absence of a full State and justifies the need of the political action of the restricted State or political society, which absorbs the representation of the common interest to undertake an economic and scalar development pathway among a World Order.

For restricted State to accomplish its political goal, a strategic principle of its economic sphere is to deploy a set of instruments to achieve its economic function of creating the favorable conditions for production and capitalist accumulation. To take advantage of backwardness, State has to channel budget policies, development banks and foreign capital to productive investments privileging industrial patterns and infrastructure where technological progress is recent and faster as well as deepen the training and qualification of the workforce to enhance their physical and cognitive strength.

Another advantage of backwardness lies in the possibility to undertake a development pathway not in a linear or classical way favored by neoclassical economics through its static equilibrium thought, but from a dynamic disequilibrium perspective, meaning a development modality through discontinuities and historical leaps. This is the economic strategy of the State focused to induce and unbalanced development by creating external economies and its complementary effects to boost industrial sectors of rapid growth favoring the expansion of national industries by granting subsidies and protection against external competition.

To achieve its objectives, State must gain a relative autonomy from dominant social groups within the Historic Bloc as well as reduce its vulnerability to the global market as opposite forces that erode the establishment of a new development modality under national premises. This means the need to relaunch relationship between State and civil society, especially with organized subaltern social classes to carry out institutional innovations that enable a new organized and controlled economic State interventionism. The building of innovative economic structures must let the State to contain the shaping of national geography by the interest of local and global investment flows and to reallocate them by national interest.

These economic principles of the role of the State to accomplish its political goal to undertake a development pathway in a backwardness condition in a certain historic stage of capitalism or time dimension correspond to a scalar accumulation strategy or space dimension. This is the State promotion to homogenize scales within national space in order to control and reduce the uneven geographical development derived from the accumulation and reproduction of capital, hence producing a regulated, functional and organized space through State's institutional–territorial apparatus.

References

Brenner, N. (2004). *New state spaces. Urban Governance and the rescaling of statehood*. New York: Oxford University Press.

Buci-Glucksmann, C. (1979). *Gramsci y el Estado. (Hacia una teoría materialista de la filosofía)*. Madrid: Siglo XXI de España editores.

Engels, F. (1989). *El origen de la familia, la propiedad privada y el estado*. México: Premia.

Evans, P. (2007). *Instituciones y desarrollo en la era de la globalización neoliberal*. Bogotá: ILSA.

Gerschenkron, A. (1968). *El atraso económico en su perspectiva histórica*. Barcelona: Ariel.

Gramsci, A. (1980). *Notas sobre Maquiavelo, sobre la política y sobre el Estado moderno*. Madrid: Nueva Visión.

Gramsci, A. (1981). *Cuadernos de la Cárcel*. México: Era.

Gramsci, A. (1996). *Note sul Machiavelli, sulla política e sullo Stato moderno*. Roma: Riuniti, Biblioteca del pensiero moderno.

Gramsci, A. (1999). *Cuadernos de la cárcel*. México: Era.
Gramsci, A. (2009). *La política y el Estado moderno*. España: Biblioteca Pensamiento Crítico.
Hirschman, A. (1964). *La estrategia del desarrollo económico*. México: Fondo de Cultura Económica.
Jessop, B. (2002). *The future of the capitalist state*. Cambridge: Polity Press.
Juanes, J. (1982). *Marx o la crítica de la Economía Política como fundamento*. Puebla: Universidad Autónoma de Puebla.
Lefebvre, H. (2003). Space and the state. In N. Brenner, B. Jessop, M. Jones, & G. Macleod (Eds.), *State/space a reader* (pp. 84–100). Malden: Blackwell Publishing.
Lefebvre, H. (2013). *La producción del espacio*. Madrid: Capitán Swing.
Lenin, V. (1978). *V.I. Lenin, Obras escogidas*. México: Progreso.
Mandel, E. (1976). Capitalism and regional disparities. *Southwest Economy and Society, 1*, 41–47.
Marx, C. (1975a). *Crítica de la filosofía del estado y del derecho de Hegel*. México: Ediciones de cultura popular.
Marx, C. (1975b). *La lucha de clases en Francia de 1848 a 1850*. México: Progreso.
Marx, C. (1982). *Introducción general a la crítica de la economía política*. México: Siglo XXI.
Marx, C. (2001). *El Capital. Crítica de la economía política*. México: Fondo de Cultura Económica.
Marx, C., & Engels, F. (1965). *Manifiesto del partido comunista*. Pekín: Ediciones en lenguas extranjeras.
Marx, C., & Engels, F. (1967). *La sagrada familia*. México: Grijalbo.
Marx, C., & Engels, F. (1970). *La ideología alemana*. Barcelona: Grijalbo.
Oliver, L. (2013). *Gramsci. La otra política. Descifrando y debatiendo los cuadernos de la cárcel*. México: Itaca.
Portanteiro, J. (1977). Gramsci y el análisis de coyuntura. *Revista Mexicana de Sociología*.
Portelli, H. (1977). *Gramsci y el Bloque Histórico*. México: Siglo XXI.
Sacristán, M. (2013). *Antonio Gramsci. Antología*. Madrid: Akal.
Soja, E. (1989). *Postmodern geographies. The reassertion of space in critical social theory*. London: Verso.

CHAPTER 3

Long-Term Cyclicality of Capitalism as State Time Dimension

Marx explains the capitalist industrial cyclicality in *Das Kapital*.[1] So-called *short, Juglar*[2] *or industrial cycles,* they relate to the replacement of fixed capital from a given productive technological base, which the evolutionist thought places as *incremental innovations,*[3] involving quantitative rather

[1] "The enormous capacity, inherent in the manufacturing system, to expand in leaps and bounds and its dependence on the world market necessarily generate feverish production and the consequent saturation of markets, which when contracting originate a period of paralysis. The life of industry becomes a sequence of periods of average animation, prosperity, overproduction, crisis and stagnation" (Marx, 2001, Volume I, Chapter XIII, p. 376) (See Diagram 3.1).

[2] Regarding to the industrial cycles, the most important work of the second half of the nineteenth century was *Des crises commerciales et de leur retour périodique en France, in Angleterre et aux Etat-Unis* by Clement Juglar published in 1862 in France. He was the first who made use of statistical series in a systematic way (mainly on prices, interest rates and central bank balance sheets) and with the precise purpose of analyzing a defined phenomenon. Furthermore, Schumpeter claims that Juglar discovered the 10-year duration of the cycle (Rodríguez, 2005, Appendix second chapter, p. 51).

[3] "Incremental innovations: These can often occur, not so much as a result of deliberate research and development activity, but as the result of inventions and improvements suggested by engineers and others directly involved in the production process, or as a result of user initiatives and proposals ("learn by doing" and "learn by using"). Although their combined effect is extremely important on productivity growth, incremental innovation does not have dramatic effects on its own, and can sometimes go unnoticed and

C. M. Sánchez Ramírez, *Knowledge Capitalism and State Theory*, Palgrave Insights into Apocalypse Economics,
https://doi.org/10.1007/978-3-030-71411-6_3

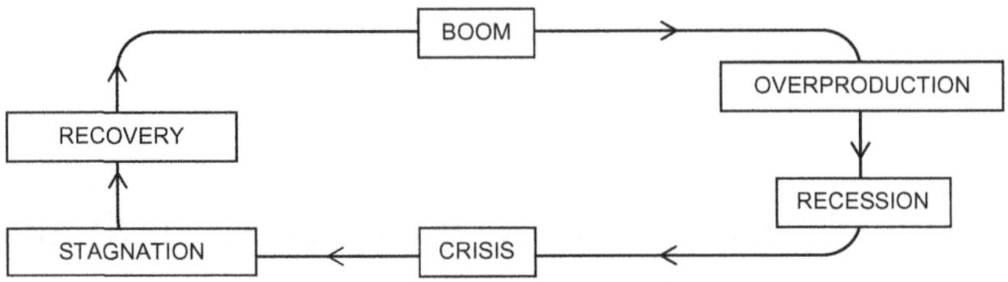

Diagram 3.1 Marx industrial cycle (*Source* Own elaboration based on Marx (2001))

than qualitative changes in technology and presenting an average duration of ten years according to Marx. At the beginning of the cycle, a significant proportion of capitals renew their fixed part and the duration of the cycle relates to the duration of the useful life of the fixed capital, coinciding with its time of circulation.

> To the same extent as the capitalist mode of production develops, the volume of value and the life span of the fixed capital employed develop, the life of industry and industrial capital develops in each particular investment, becoming a life of many years, say ten, on average. If, on the one hand, the development of fixed capital prolongs this life, on the other, it is shortened by the constant disruption of the means of production, which also constantly increases as the capitalist mode of production develops. Hence, with this development, the change in the means of production and the need to continually replenish them also increases, as a result of moral wear and tear, long before they have physically exhausted their lives. It can be assumed that for the most decisive branches of large industry this life cycle is now, on average, ten years. (Marx, 2001, Volume II, Chapter IX, p. 165)

Based on Marx and Juglar analysis of short or industrial cycles and on the recognition of the nature of the crisis as a periodic and organically inherent phenomenon in the capitalist system, Kondratiev was one of the first non-strictly Marxist scholars, although not the only one, to study the long-term cyclicality of capitalism (Sandoval, 2008). He focused on

unregistered. However, its effects are evident in the continued growth of productivity" (Freeman & Perez, 1988, pp. 45–46).

international economic dynamics after WWI and in the crisis period, understanding it as a "rupture of the equilibrium in a changing system of elements of the national or world economy" that occurs particularly at the beginning of the second decade of the twentieth century, caused by "a disproportionate distribution of productive force and purchasing power," expressed in the contradictions between supply and demand of products in the world market. To approach the study of capitalist dynamics, which implies prolonged and deep economic fluctuations, he proposes the existence of long cycles as a methodological approach.

However, unlike other contemporary scholars in whom he does not recognize a clear and determined approach to the characteristics of the course of long cycles, Kondratiev carries out a statistical analysis from the data processing of a set of industrialized countries of the time: Germany, France, England and the United States. In this way, taking into account the average price level, the interest rate, the nominal wage, the transit of foreign trade, the extraction and consumption of coal, as well as the production of iron and lead, he concludes that the dynamics of the previous elements reveal the existence of long cycles that contain ascending and descending periods. Recognizing that although his study focuses on characterizing the long cyclicality of the capitalist mode of production, it does not address the question of its causes.

For this, Kondratiev considers necessary the study of capitalism in its "concrete features" and not only statistical, but also descriptive, so that in the development of long cycles he locates four "empirical regularities." The first of them manifests itself before the beginning of an ascending period of each long cycle, by observing profound changes in the technique of production and exchange, preceded by considerable technical inventions and discoveries, as well as changes in the conditions of monetary circulation and the strengthening of the role of new countries in world economic life. The second regularity relates to the observation during the ascending periods, of a greater number of social upheavals, revolutions and wars, in comparison with the descending periods of the long cycles. The third empirical regularity is the prolonged depression in agriculture, during the downdraft periods, and finally observes that the economic dynamics of long cycles is similar to those of short cycles, presenting stages of boom, crisis and depression as shown in Diagram 3.2 described in Table 3.1.

Hence, Kondratiev deduces that during the descending period of the long cycle, the short cycles would be characterized by presenting longer

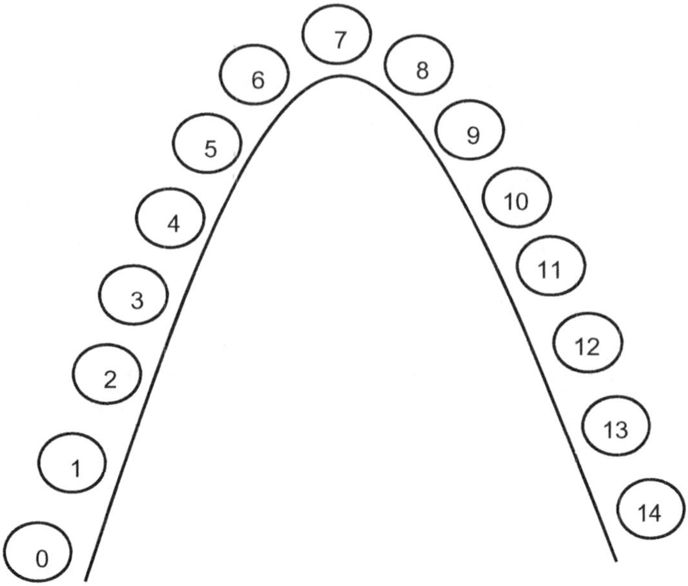

Diagram 3.2 Dynamics of Kondratiev long cycles (*Source* Own elaboration based on Sandoval (2008))

and deeper depression stages, while the boom stages would be shorter and weaker, observing the opposite features in the short cycle during the upward periods of the long cycle. From this analysis proposes a capitalism periodization of two and a half long cycles, with a duration that fluctuates between 47 and 60 years after the industrial revolution as shown in Fig. 3.1.

After Kondratiev, but also motivated by understanding a crisis situation of capitalism, particularly the one that takes place in the mid-sixties of the twentieth century, Mandel (1986) emphasizes the need to incorporate in Marxist analysis, the theory of long waves in order to account for significant turning points throughout the economic history of the capitalist mode of production. In controversy with Kondratiev, Mandel argues that long waves are the product of fluctuations in the rate of profit, expressed in the growth of industrial production and the world market. The first as a variable that captures the long-term trend of capitalist production and the second as one that marks the rate of expansion of the world market,

Table 3.1 Dynamics of Kondratiev long cycles

0	– Renovation and expansion of basic capital goods, radical modifications and regrouping of the basic productive forces of society
	– Huge capital expenditures
	– Increasing accumulation and disposition of physical and monetary capital; development of the financial system
1	– Application of accumulated technical investments
2	– Growth of productive forces
3	– Struggle for new raw materials markets
4	– Expansion of the world market
5	– Fight against obsolete socio-economic relationships that hold back development
6	– Wars and social struggles
7	– The inflection point occurs when the demand for capital exceeds its accumulation curve, making capital more expensive and increasing the interest rate
	– The pace of investment in large-scale projects falls, economic activity slows and prices fall
8	– Starts the search for ways to reduce production costs and for new technical innovations
9	– Interest rate growth slows
	– The investments reduce and the demand for capital over its supply decreases
10	– Starts a process of capital accumulation in the hands of banking, commercial and industrial companies
11	– Agriculture experiences a deeper depression than industry, due to the fall in the demand for raw materials for the production process
12	– The curve of the rate of capital accumulation increasingly exceeds the investment curve, making capital cheaper
13	– Due to the declining prices, gold mining is more profitable, increasing the influx of new gold
14	– Favorable conditions for a new upward period

Source Own elaboration based on Sandoval (2008)

thus disqualifying the use of commodity prices used by Kondratiev in calculating the long cycles.

In Mandel's conception, during the expansive stage of the long wave, the rate of profit would increase due to the decrease in the organic composition of capital, the increase in the rate of surplus value, the fall in the prices of constant capital and the decrease in capital turnover time. This is mainly because of a set of exogenous factors (subjective, extra-economic and/or the relative autonomy of the class struggle) that cause the behavior of the previous variables. In the depressive stage,

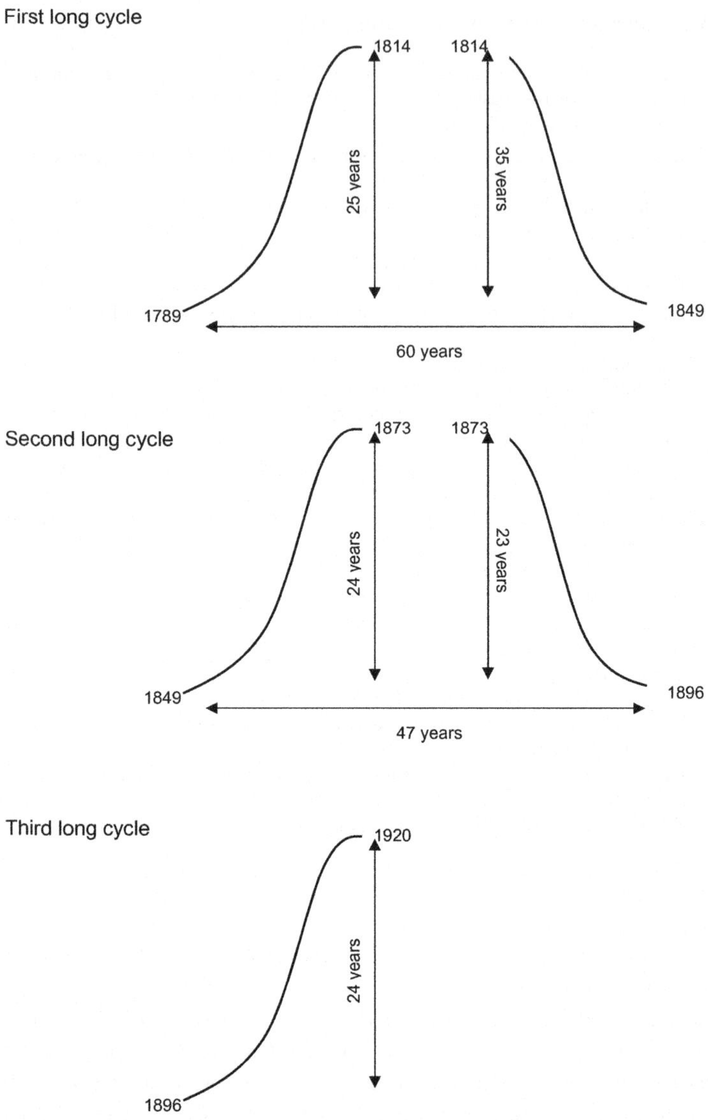

Fig. 3.1 Kondratiev long cycles (*Source* Own elaboration based on Sandoval (2008))

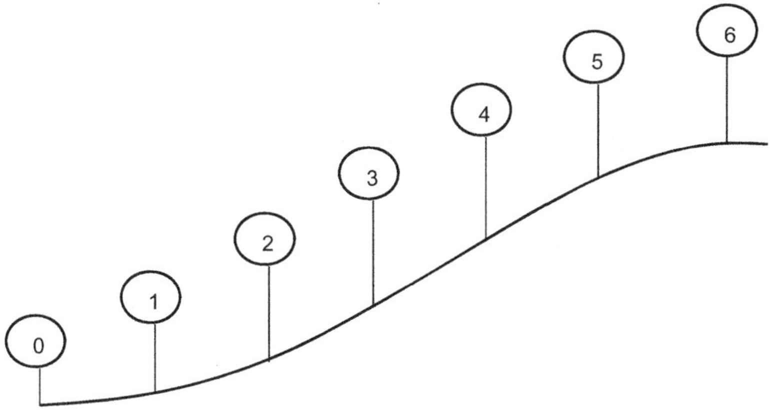

Diagram 3.3 Dynamics of Mandel rising long wave (*Source* Own elaboration based on Mandel (1986))

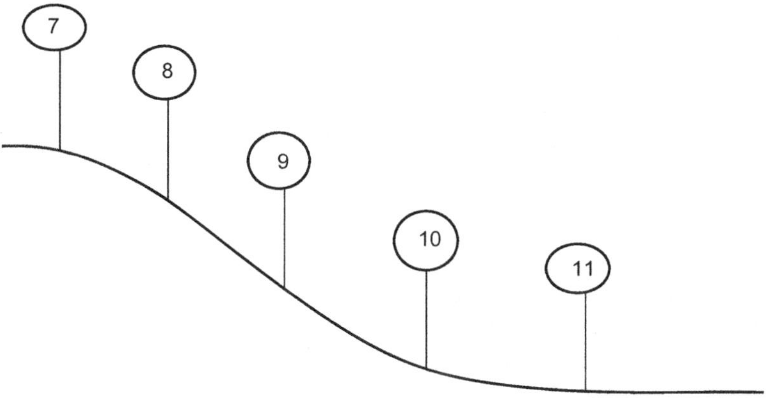

Diagram 3.4 Dynamics of Mandel declining long wave (*Source* Own elaboration based on Mandel (1986))

the variables involved would have the opposite behavior, but derived from endogenous factors, and the lack of investment would drive the accumulation of capital-money that will drive the next technological revolution. Diagrams 3.3 and 3.4 and Tables 3.2 and 3.3 show the main characteristics of both rising and declining stages of the long wave.

Table 3.2 Dynamics of Mandel rising long wave

0	– Extra-economic factors such as wars of conquest, expansion and contraction of capital scope, inter-capitalist competition, class struggle, revolutions, counterrevolutions, etc.
1	– Rise in profit expectations and profit realization
2	– Rise in the accumulation rate of productive capital (investment)
3	– Technological revolution characterized by a radical revision of the basic techniques used in all spheres of capitalist production and distribution
4	– Readjusting of labor managing and direction
5	– Fight against obsolete socio-economic relationships that hold back development
6	– Long-term rise in the average rate of profit caused by a high increase in the rate of surplus value, a strong deceleration in the rate of increase in the organic composition of capital and a high acceleration in the circulation of capital

Source Own elaboration based on Mandel (1986)

Table 3.3 Dynamics of Mandel declining long wave

7	– Long-term fall in the average rate of profit caused by a low or no increase in the rate of surplus value, a weak or no deceleration in the rate of increase in the organic composition of capital and a low acceleration in the circulation of capital
8	– Decrease in profit expectations and profit realization
9	– Decrease in the accumulation rate of productive capital (investment)
10	– Contraction in industrial production and world exports
11	– Fall in real wages

Source Own elaboration based on Mandel (1986)

Mandel considers technological change as a distinctive feature between a long wave and another and focuses on the emergence of a new driving force that represents the decisive dynamic element of the industrial complex.

> The fundamental revolutions of energy technology – the production technology of the driving forces by means of machines – stands as the fundamental moments of technological revolutions as a whole. The machined production of steam engines since 1848. The mechanized production of electric and internal combustion motors in the last decade of the nineteenth century. The mechanized production of nuclear powered apparatus electronically organized since the forties of this century. Represent the three great technological revolutions engendered in the capitalist mode of production since the 'original' industrial revolution in the late eighteenth

> century. When a technological revolution takes place in the production of motorized machines by means of machinery, then the entire system of machines progressively transforms. (Mandel, 1979, p. 115)

In a similar way to the *empirical regularity* with which Kondratiev links the economic dynamics of long cycles with that of short cycles, Mandel argues that these "long waves" articulate with the "classical cycles." During the expansion period of the long wave, industrial cycle boom periods will be longer and intensive and cyclical overproduction crises will be shorter and superficial. When declining tendency prevails in long waves, industrial cycle boom periods will be less feverish and shorter, while the classic overproduction crisis periods will be longer and deeper.

Based on the discussion above, Mandel explains the history of capitalism as a succession of cyclical movements of approximately fifty years. Since they do not have an absolute rhythm or regularity, he locates four periods or long waves of capitalist development: a first period from the late eighteenth century to 1847, characterized by steam-powered manufacturing in the most important branches of industry and industrial countries, a second period after 1847 and until the beginning of the last decade of the nineteenth century, characterized by the emergence and expansion of steam engine machinery, as the main motorized machine, a third period from the end of the nineteenth century to the beginning of WWII, characterized by the widespread application of internal combustion and electric engines in all branches of industry and finally a fourth period from 1940, characterized by the control of machines by electronic devices, as well as by the gradual introduction of atomic energy.

In contrast to previous studies, and from the evolutionary thought influenced by Charles Darwin, Schumpeter (1997) argued that historical change is a process of social development, not necessarily circular and transformed by *historical individuals* in time. In controversy with Mandel, Schumpeter states that development is the change in economic life not imposed on it from the outside. That is, it is not caused by exogenous factors, but has an internal origin from a position without development, where the necessary conditions have been previously created, qualifying it as a phenomenon opposed to the trend toward neoclassical equilibrium.

In Schumpeterian development, spontaneous and discontinuous alterations appear mainly in the sphere of industrial and commercial life, but not in the sphere of consumer needs for finished products; it is the producer who initiates economic change, even "educating" consumers, teaching them to need new products or products that differ somewhat from existing ones. Schumpeter defines the activity of producing as the combination of materials and forces that are within our reach, so that spontaneous alterations in economic development represent new combinations of productive means; that is, development is the implementation of innovations[4]—the use of the existing resources in a distinctive way—in the industrial and commercial spheres. These innovations neither distribute evenly over time nor randomly throughout the economic system, but rather emerge in clusters concentrating in certain sectors.

A central contribution of Schumpeterian evolutionism is the importance of the financial sphere as a catalyst for new combinations or innovations. The availability of the means of production to carry out the new combinations is a central problem of the entrepreneur as the agent that carries them out. For this reason, credit, and in particular the money obtained from the creation of purchasing power by banks, takes on special importance in a situation of backwardness, where there is no result from the prior development to innovate, that is, the growth of the social savings and the annually free resources.

In this idea of the importance of financing the entrepreneur from bank credit in an underdeveloped position, Schumpeter agrees with Gerschenkron on the central role played by German banks in the industrialization process of the European country. In this way, the banker becomes another historical individual, a capitalist who owns money, rights over money or material goods, and is willing to invest in new combinations—*authorizing men in the name of society to carry them out*—an owner of productive means. Banker clearly distinguishes from entrepreneur as the latter is the individual in charge of directing the new combinations and capable of stamping his historical seal in time, providing the society with a new lifestyle.

[4]These innovations include the next. (1) The introduction of a new product or a new quality of the same product. (2) The introduction of a new production method, which does not need to be based on a new discovery from a scientific point of view, and may simply consist of a new way of a merchandise commercial manage. (3) The opening of a new market in which a special branch of manufacturing has not entered, despite the fact that said market previously existed. (4) The conquest of a new source of supply of raw materials or semi-manufactured goods. (5) The creation of a new organization of any industry, such as a monopoly position or the cancellation of a previously existing monopoly position (Schumpeter, 1997, p. 77).

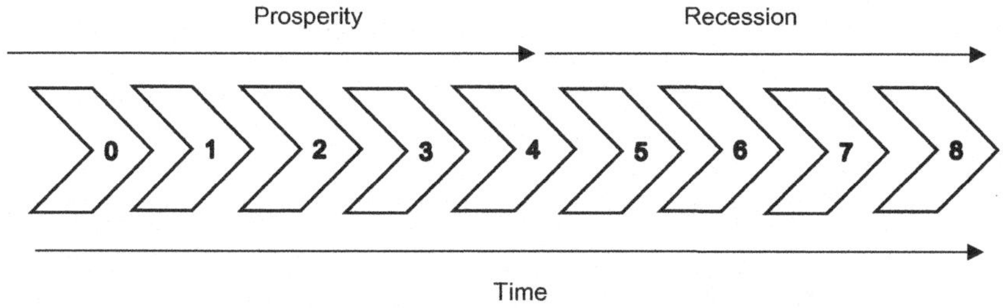

Diagram 3.5 Sequence of Schumpeterian economic development (*Source* Own elaboration based on Schumpeter (2002))

In his analysis of economic development, Schumpeter does not confer much importance to inventions or technological change, stating that they have no economic preponderance while not put into practice by the entrepreneur. Entrepreneur's innovations do not need to be inventions. They can simply involve the different uses of the available productive means of the economic system, transforming the economic sphere for several decades, promoting development. Instead, Schumpeter highlights the leadership of the business agent in overcoming resistance to change from groups threatened by innovation, subsequently obtaining their cooperation, and ultimately gaining the trust of consumers.

In a first simple approach to model the sequence of economic development, Schumpeter considers a cycle with two stages: prosperity and recession as shown in Diagram 3.5 and described in Table 3.4. Meanwhile to perform a historical analysis presents three long cycles: the first one that of the industrial revolution from 1780 to 1842, the second one that of the steam and steel from 1842 to 1897 and finally the third one that of the electricity, chemistry and automobiles from 1898 onwards.

Inspired by the theory of economic development of Schumpeterian evolutionism, Perez (2004) develops a framework for analyzing the long-term cyclicality of capitalism around the concept of *wave of development*, with special emphasis on the dynamic relationship between the spheres of productive capital and financial capital, to which Schumpeter assigned a central role in economic development. In a similar way to Schumpeterian historical individuals, productive capital encompasses the motivations and behavior of the agents that generate new wealth, producing goods or providing services. Meanwhile financial capital represents the criteria and

Table 3.4 Characteristics of Schumpeterian economic development sequence

<table>
<tr><td rowspan="2">Prosperity</td><td>0. Increase of knowledge</td><td>1. Induce the entrepreneur to undertake something new, borrowing money to build his factory and equipment</td><td>2. Other entrepreneurs follow along the path of innovation</td></tr>
<tr><td colspan="2">3. The total output of the economy increases until new products from entrepreneurs hit the market</td><td>4. Old companies face a new source of imbalance</td></tr>
<tr><td rowspan="2">Recession</td><td colspan="2">5. Over time, business activity slows down and stops, as its possibilities are limited. Eventually competition eliminates benefits, exhausting the innovative drive</td><td>6. Furthermore, innovation upsets the balance. Which means fluctuations and successive attempts to adapt to changing temporal situations</td></tr>
<tr><td colspan="2">7. Adaptation to the new created situation. Elimination of what is unable to adapt. Reabsorption of the innovation results in the system. Reorganization of economic life</td><td>8. Given conditions for a new beginning of innovation</td></tr>
</table>

Source Own elaboration based on Schumpeter (2002)

behavior of agents who possess wealth in the form of money and other paper values.

Freeman and Perez (1988) argue that each wave is founded on a new *techno-economic paradigm* that arises from the previous one and shows its advantages during the descending phase of the wave. This paradigm establishes a dominant technological regime only after a structural adjustment crisis that in turn implies profound social and institutional changes, as well as the replacement of driving branches of the economy during several decades.

Thus, in the long-term cyclicality of the capitalist system proposed by Perez, the *big-bang* heralds a new wave. Opening up a new technological revolution, driven by the role of financial capital that catalyzes the new revolution in the irruption process during the wave installing stage until the productive capital takes the leadership in the stage of deployment or synergy (see Diagram 3.6; Table 3.5). This is, between financial capital—that enables and speeds up the technological revolution—and productive capital—as the ultimate wealth producer—molding the institutions of a world that will come later.

From the above analysis, Perez (2004) presents five waves of the capitalist system: a first wave from 1771 to 1828, marked by the industrial technological revolution in England; a second wave that originated in England from 1829 to 1874, characterized by the era of the steam engine and the railways, and spread to Europe and the United States; a third wave from 1875 to 1907 in the United States and Germany, the age of

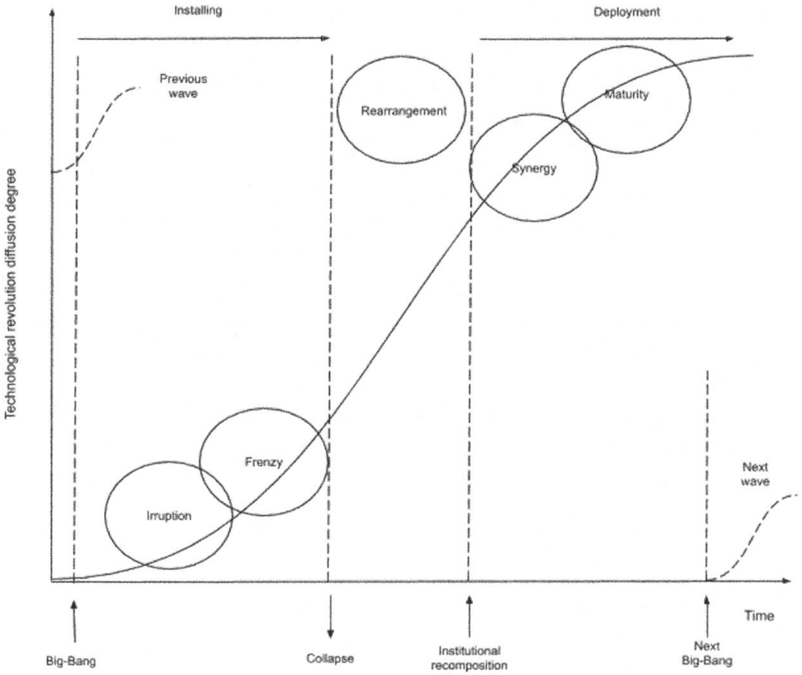

Diagram 3.6 Installing and deployment of Perez capitalism wave of development (*Source* Own elaboration based on Perez (2004))

steel and heavy engineering; the fourth wave that originated in the United States and spread to Europe from 1908 to 1970, marked by the era of oil, automobiles and mass production and finally a fifth wave that began in 1971 in the United States and spread to Europe and Asia, characterized by the era of information technology and telecommunications.

Gramsci's theoretical contribution to the understanding of the long-term cyclicality of capitalism founds again in the articulation between the economic structure and a set of superstructure spheres that synthesize in the State. Thus,

> When studying a historical period one sees the great importance of this distinction: there is a crisis, which sometimes lasts for several decades. This

Table 3.5 Stages characteristics of Perez wave of development

Installing	Irruption	New technological revolution attracts financial capital Intensive financing of new technologies Disregard for traditional assets
	Frenzy	Decoupling between financial capital and productive capital Financial bubble Increasing gap between real and paper assets
Rearrangement		The resulting collapses from frenzy can create the conditions for the State to establish regulations, turning the game in favor of productive capital and leading to a period of more harmonious growth
Deployment	Sinergy	Recoupling between financial capital and productive capital Productive capital takes the helm Recoupling between real and paper assets Consistent growth
	Maturity	Signs of detachment Decreasing investment opportunities "Idle money" moving into new areas, sectors and regions

Source: Own elaboration based on Perez (2004)

> means that insurmountable contradictions have been revealed in the structure, that the political forces that operate positively for the preservation of the structure itself are nevertheless reinforced by alleviating within certain limits. These incessant and persevering efforts (since no social force wants to confess ever that has been overcome) form the terrain of the "casual" about the forces "trying" to prove (to the facts in the final analysis, that is organized with its own triumph, but immediately through the ideological, religious, philosophical, political, legal controversy, etc.) that "the necessary and sufficient conditions already exist so that certain tasks can and therefore must be resolved historically". (Gramsci, 1999, C.4, paragraph 38)

That is, in a situation of economic–structural exhaustion or historical crisis, the set of political forces organized around the State in a restricted sense make all the efforts that are within their power to maintain the "established order". "... and the State represents all attempts to permanently crystallize a certain phase of development, a situation" (Gramsci, 1971, p. 158). Meanwhile, material conditions already found in the field of the structure allow a new solution to the social conflict expressing through the different planes that correspond to the superstructure of civil society, opening the way toward a hegemonic construction that contributes a new common sense to the world.

Marx explains those material conditions that open up a new phase of development when analyzing machinery and large industry in *Das Kapital*

> Upon reaching a certain degree of development, large industry also came into conflict on a technical level with its artisanal and manufacturing base. Increasing dimensions of the driving machines, the transmission mechanisms and the machine tools; greater complication, multiform and more exact precision of its components, as the machine tool emancipated itself from the artisan mode that had originally dominated its construction and acquired a free figure, determined only by its mechanical purpose; improvement of the automatic system and the increasingly inevitable use of a material that is more difficult to master, for example iron, instead of wood; the solution of all these problems, which arose as a result of a natural process, was everywhere met with individual limitations, which even the combined labor force in manufacturing only exceeded in degree, but not in substance. The manufactory could not supply machines like the modern printing press, the modern steam loom, and the modern carding machine. (Marx, 2001, Volume I, Chapter XIII, p. 329)

As the machine tool is the part of the machinery that acts on the work object, it substitutes the action of man. From being the hands of man that act on the work object, machine tools become the intermediary between man and the work object. Thus, derived from a technological revolution, a *radical evolution* of machine tools manages to modify a part of the set of machinery, constituting a new technological base that changes direction and manage of labor as Mandel states in the rising long wave dynamics. The articulation of the new technological base with the emerging form of labor organization in the production process represents a technological–productive basement that takes to an industrial revolution.

These innovations, both in the radical evolution of machine tools and in the organization and manage of labor, tend to concentrate in certain sectors as Schumpeter argues, establishing a set of driving branches of

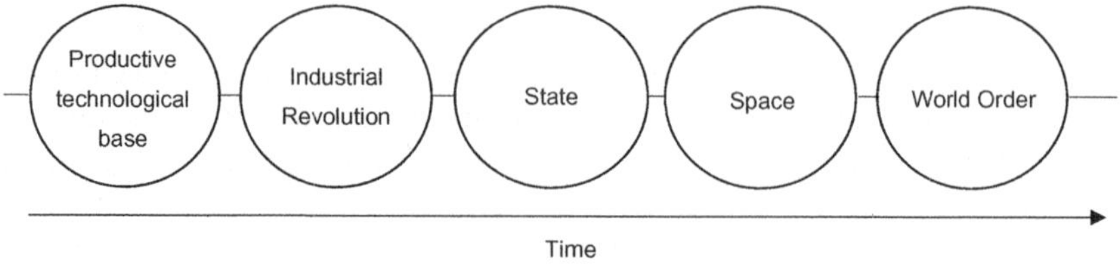

Diagram 3.7 Gramsci's phase of development: economic structure and socio-space-institutional fabric (*Source* Own elaboration)

the economy or industrial pattern, articulating the other sectors and influencing the economic cycle. These material conditions contribute to what Gramsci calls the solution to the social conflict, implying deep institutional changes as Perez states. Thus, the superstructure or socio-space-institutional fabric bases on the economic structure as a set of political, ideological, cultural and institutional fields of action of the subjects or Historic Bloc, where the economy determines the other social spheres. Meanwhile, in the field of politics, the superstructure construction or institutional change corresponds to a certain form of State and an International System of States Hegemony or World Order. Under the Hegemony of a superpower, it projects its national solution or development pathway to the others, configuring a geographic pattern of uneven development.

Therefore, a phase of development comprises the new historic economic structure in terms of the capitalism long-term cyclicality, meaning the time dimension of the socio-space-institutional construction synthesized in a State form, which also has its own dynamics and an active role, becoming necessary and functional to the economic structure (see Diagram 3.7).

3.1 Rise of a New Phase of Development Under Neoliberalism in the United States

Fordism–Keynesian phase of development consolidates in the United States around 1935, having as a structural economic foundation the development of mechanical engineering of interchangeable parts and Fordism as an organization and managing labor mode. Meanwhile, the socio-space-institutional fabric synthesized in the welfare State, as a representation of the social interest to maintain the workers' health in optimal conditions for the continuous reproduction of their physical strength. The dynamics of the economic cycle from the increase in aggregate demand had been successful after the Great Depression. However, in the course of subsequent decades, the industrial profit rate performed a decreasing trend as shown in Fig. 3.2 caused by the structural economic exhaustion of the development phase.

Since the profit rate is:

$$\text{Profit rate} = \frac{\text{Surplus value}}{\text{Constant Capital} + \text{Variable Capital}} \tag{1}$$

$$\text{Surplus value} = f(\text{Productivity}) = f(\text{Technology, Worker training, Labor managing}) \tag{2}$$

In addition, surplus value is a function of productivity that depends on technology development, worker training and qualification, and labor organization and management, all of them are structural variables located in the numerator of Eq. 1, in a direct relation to the rate of profit.

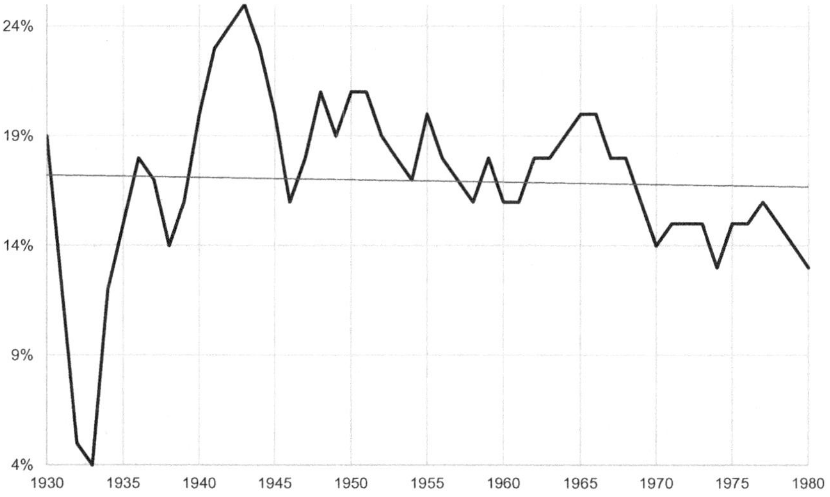

Fig. 3.2 United States industrial profit rate 1930–1980 (*Source* Own elaboration with data from the Bureau of Economic Analysis of the U.S. Department of Commerce)

The material limits of the automotive, metal-mechanic and petrochemical driving branches, based on mechanical engineering and Fordist organization, would impose a decrease in the productivity of workers and consequently the decreasing impact on the trend of the industrial profit rate.

Moreover, in the face of labor falling productivity, workers spent more time making the same product than before. The increase in the amount of time occupied in the sphere of production meant an increase in the disbursement of wages to the workers by the capitalist, as well as an increase in the investment of fixed capital to replace the deteriorated machinery used longer, finally causing the increasing time and value in the manufacture of a commodity. These increases in time and value increased prices in the market causing inflation and deepening the falling trend of the profit rate, derived from the inverse relation of constant and variable capital with the profit rate, expressed in Eq. 1. In sum, the depletion of the economic structural elements of the Fordist-Keynesian phase of development would have led to the economic phenomenon known as stagflation during the seventies of the twentieth century.

However, the Keynesian macroeconomic toolkit was limited to solve the double process of economic stagnation and increased inflation or stagflation due to its priority focus on increasing aggregate demand as a strategy for boosting the economic cycle. In order to do this, from a given situation of "equilibrium" between the liquidity preference-money supply (LM) and the investment-savings (IS) curves (point A in Fig. 3.3) the Federal Reserve or Central Bank applied an expansionary monetary police, decreasing the interest rate to boost investment and production. This is the transit from LM_1 to LM_2 that established a new long-run aggregate supply or production target to expand the goods and service market curve (IS) (point B in Fig. 3.4).

The expected effects of this expansionary monetary policy is to get a new equilibrium in the economy (point C in Fig. 3.5), with the transit from IS_1 to IS_2, meaning the expansion of the national product and the expected increase of the interest rate to counteract the inflation. Nevertheless, the economic structure limits had left little room for innovation inhibiting the expansion of demand; meanwhile, the monetary policy tended to worsen the economic paralysis and inflation, configuring a crisis of over investment and production. In this way, the Keynesian macroeconomic framework faced a dilemma: An expansionary monetary policy was

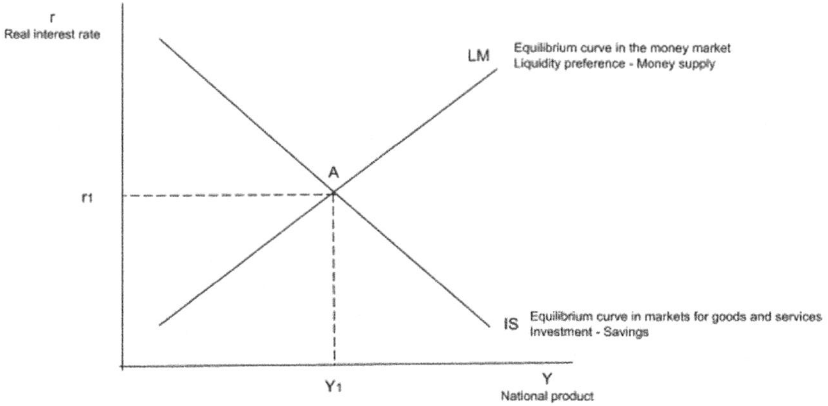

Fig. 3.3 Keynesian macroeconomic equilibrium between liquidity preference-money supply (LM) and the investment-savings (IS) curves (*Source* Own elaboration based on IS–LM equilibrium model)

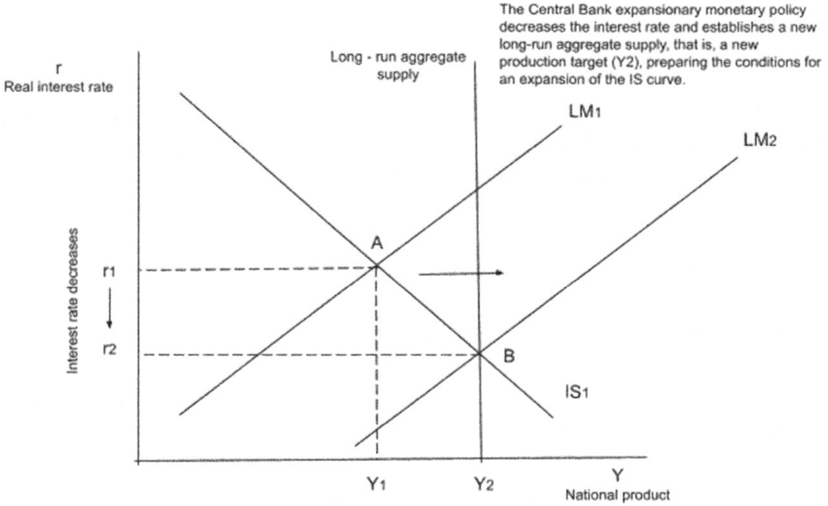

Fig. 3.4 Keynesian macroeconomic expansionary monetary policy (*Source* Own elaboration based on IS–LM equilibrium model)

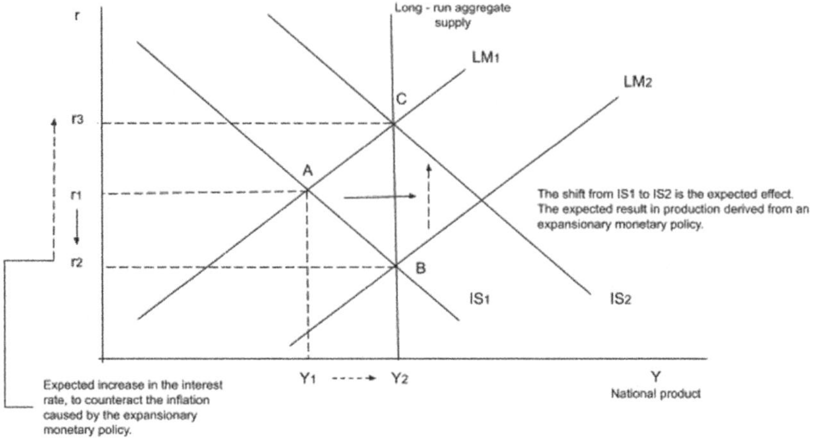

Fig. 3.5 Keynesian macroeconomic expansionary monetary policy expected effects (*Source* Own elaboration based on IS–LM equilibrium model)

not boosting output but inflation and a contractionary monetary policy did not slow down inflation but economic growth.

The solution to the Keynesian dilemma was in the emergence of a new economic structure founded in the microprocessor and software development as technological revolution and the transition from Fordism to Toyotism as an innovative organization and managing labor mode that takes advantage of the labor cognitive and creative capabilities. The first mover to embrace the benefits of the emerging technological revolution was the financial capital through mortgage securitization.

During the eighties of the twentieth century, investment banks such as Salomon Brothers, Merrill Lynch, Fidelity and Vanguard among others created new methods to securitize mortgages. Using computing and probability software, investment banks combined a large number of mortgages in a common deposit in order to structure them as securities to sell them on the stock market. In a set of thousands of mortgages, banks evaluate the flow of payments statistically, estimating the probability that a certain number of mortgages will fall into one of these categories: solvent, delayed or insolvent, opening up the door to speculation. Risk insurance companies such as AIG, MBLA or Ambac joined this process to reduce risk in the securities prime and subprime sections, finally submitting them to risk assessment agencies such as Moody's, Standard & Poor's and Fitch. Thanks to the structuring in sections and insurance, investment agencies could grant the highest solvency to mediocre loans, increasing speculation.

Investments banks also took advantage from stagflation. The Glass-Steagall law approved by the U.S. Congress in 1933 regulated commercial banks, establishing a federal deposit insurance covering deposits up to one hundred dollars in 1980. Moreover, Congress allowed the Federal Reserve to set a limit on the interest rate that commercial banks could pay to savers. This rule known as Regulation Q also intended to ensure that competition for deposits among banking institutions did not get out of control. However, during the second half of the sixties, inflation began to rise, pushing up interest rates. Rates that banks paid to other banks for overnight loans had rarely exceeded 6% in the decades before 1980, when it reached 20%. Due to Regulation Q, commercial banks were required to offer just under 6% on most deposits.

That was an unsustainable restriction for depository institutions, which could not compete at the most basic level of the interest rate offered on a deposit with investment banks, which were out of the influence sphere of Glass-Steagall and Regulation Q. Through the securitization process, investment banks created funds paying higher interest rates than those that commercial banks could pay because of regulation, thus persuading consumers and businesses to abandon traditional banks for higher returns, even though the federal deposit insurance did not protect these funds. Shadow Banking System emerged this way, as a less regulated capital market growing alongside the traditional banking system.

Assets in money market mutual funds jumped from 3 billion dollars in 1977, to more than 740 billion dollars in 1995, and 1.8 trillion dollars in 2000 (Financial Crisis Inquiry Commission, 2011). This increasing funding capacity of the investment banks from the eighties enabled Schumpeterian entrepreneurs settled on San Francisco Bay area through venture capitals to innovate in the conception and design of products around the electronic and telecommunications technologies that took advantage from the valorization of creativity and transdisciplinary knowledge of labor summarized in the invention of microprocessor and software development. This neo-Schumpeterian irruption stage where financial capital boosts productive capital brought a new impulse to the profit rate, increasing productivity and surplus value, thus establishing a new technological-productive basement founded on microprocessor and software technological revolution, articulated with an organization and managing labor mode able to profit from a creative and better skilled and well-educated worker than the Fordist "trained gorilla," meaning Toyotism.

Silicon Valley entrepreneurs and California creative industries together with venture capitals emerged as a new ruling classes in the Historic Bloc. They led a hegemonic process incorporating a set of social groups: Afro-Americans, Latinos, young people, as well as social movements: feminism, anti-racism, multiculturalism, environmentalism and gay lesbian, around the cancelation of the redistributive role of the State in favor of the market as a more efficient agent for the distribution of social resources. The social remnants of the exhausted old productive technological base of Fordism–Keynesian phase of development went to the background. These were industries associated with the automotive, metal-mechanic and petrochemical driving branches: military, manufacturing and extractive industries, small enterprises and their associated financial capital, as well as social groups: evangelical Christians, southern white population and small town and rural population, white working classes and social movements: nationalist, racist and homophobic (Fraser, 2017).

This Historic Bloc founded in the electronic and telecommunications technologies industrial revolution and the efficiency of the free market as a theoretical and ideology mainstream opened up a new phase of development or Knowledge Capitalism under neoliberalism as its main Atlantic-hegemonic development pathway. Neoliberalism tended to design a Ricardian world, splitting the production sphere between product conception and design in developed scales and product manufacturing and assembly in developing regions or a—*Designed in California assembled in China*—inter-industrial and global division of labor, thus configuring an uneven geographical development pattern expressed on eminent neoliberal economic integration processes such as NAFTA (reconfigured today as USMCA Agreement) and the European Union (see Diagram 3.8).

Through the development of telecommunications making possible the global scale, neoliberal international financial flows promoted the virtual space as a new scale in this historic time of capitalism or phase of development, eroding the geography of the State while privileging the integration of the local scales with the supranational without the mediation of the national. The deployment of this new economic structure under the *glocal*

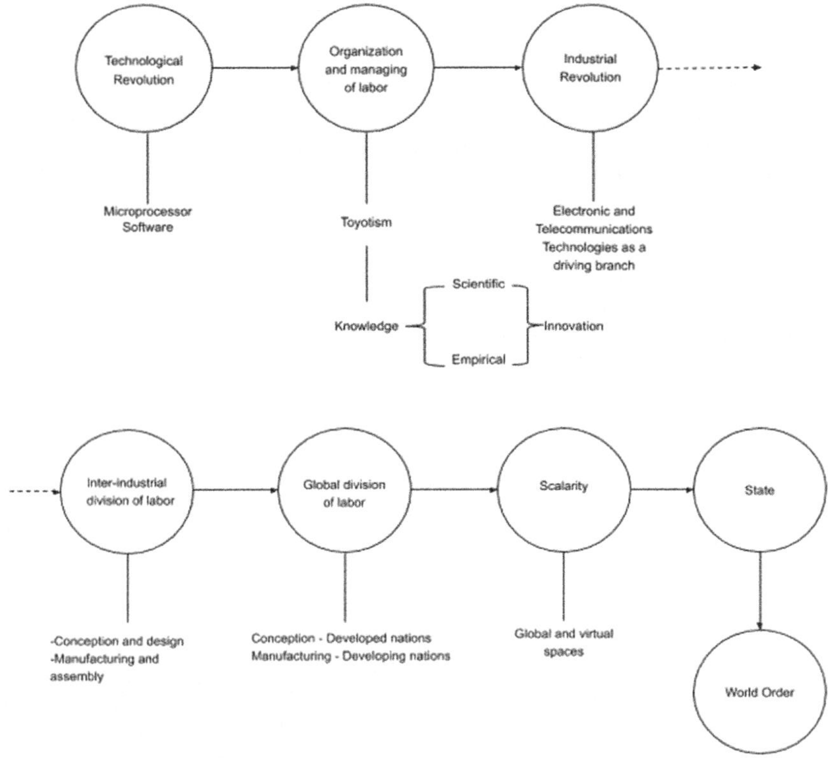

Diagram 3.8 Economic structure and articulation with socio-space-institutional fabric in Knowledge Capitalism (*Source* Own elaboration)

scalar logic of the neoliberal development pathway in the United States explains the rise of southwestern scales such as Silicon Valley, linked to the electronic and telecommunications technologies, as well as the decline of the Rust Belt in the northeast that settled activities of the automotive and metal-mechanic industrial complex. This includes cities like Chicago or Detroit: the latter headquarter of the Big Three: Ford, Chrysler and General Motors, today in decadence.

After 1980, Neoliberalism reversed the falling trend of the profit rate in the United States, although without reaching rates higher than 19% as in the previous phase of development. However, the uncontrolled growth of the financial capital over the productive one reflected in the rise of the Shadow Banking System around the preponderance of the market as a better resources distributor via financialization caused the financial-productive crisis of 2008 or *market failure*, thus preventing the subsequent deployment of the economic structure expressed in the stagnation of the industrial profit rate, which in 2019 was practically at the same level as in 2009 as shown in Fig. 3.6.

Furthermore, neoclassicism as neoliberalism theoretical matrix is limited in its analytical framework to provide an explanation of the historical change from technological development in its articulation with the socio-space-institutional fabric, as observed as follows in the Solow-Swan equation of growth rate of capital per efficient unit of labor.

Defining capital growth rate:

$$\dot{K}_t = sF(K_t, L_t, A_t) - \delta K_t \tag{3}$$

Defining capital per efficient unit of labor:

$$\widehat{K} = \frac{K}{LA} \tag{4}$$

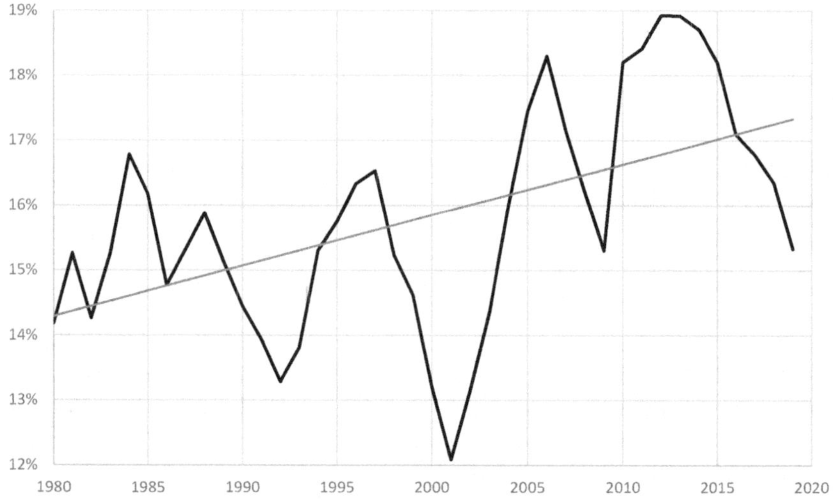

Fig. 3.6 United States industrial profit rate 1980–2019 (*Source* Own elaboration with data from the Bureau of Economic Analysis of the U.S. Department of Commerce)

Defining efficient unit of labor:

$$\widehat{L} = LA \tag{5}$$

Dividing (3) by (5):

$$\frac{\dot{K}}{\widehat{L}} = sf\left(\widehat{k}\right) - \delta\widehat{k} \tag{6}$$

Deriving capital per efficient unit of labor (Eq. 4) with respect to time:

$$\frac{\mathrm{d}\hat{K}}{\mathrm{d}t} = \frac{\mathrm{d}\left(\frac{K}{LA}\right)}{\mathrm{d}t} = \frac{LAK - K(L\dot{A} + A\dot{L})}{(LA)^2} = \frac{LA\dot{K} - KL\dot{A} - KA\dot{L}}{(LA)^2}$$
$$= \frac{\dot{K}}{LA} - \frac{K}{LA}\left(\frac{\dot{A}}{A}\right) - \frac{K}{LA}\left(\frac{\dot{L}}{L}\right)$$

Substituting $\frac{\dot{K}}{LA}$ with Eq. 6; $\left(\frac{\dot{A}}{A}\right)$ with x as technological growth rate; and $\left(\frac{\dot{L}}{L}\right)$ with n as population growth rate:

$$\frac{\mathrm{d}\widehat{K}}{\mathrm{d}t} = sf\left(\widehat{k}\right) - \delta\widehat{k} - \widehat{k}x - \widehat{k}n$$

$$\frac{\mathrm{d}\widehat{K}}{\mathrm{d}t} = sf\left(\widehat{k}\right) - (\delta + x + n)\widehat{k} \tag{7}$$

Plotting Eq. 7.

The conclusion of the neoclassical perspective of analysis from static equilibrium is that the growth rate of capital per efficient unit of labor tends to deplete in the long term. Since the transfer of the saving curve up and to the right toward a new point of equilibrium would require a decisive action by the State, particularly in backward countries, something inconceivable under the neoclassical paradigm, the alternatives available in the model to prolong the fatal destiny of economic stagnation as long as possible are found in reducing industrial activity from the reduction of capital depreciation, reducing the rate of population growth and/or stopping technological development (see Fig. 3.7).

The gap between productive and financial capitals has recently tended to deepen because of the quantitative easing strategies applied via market by the U. S. Federal Reserve and the European Union and Japan

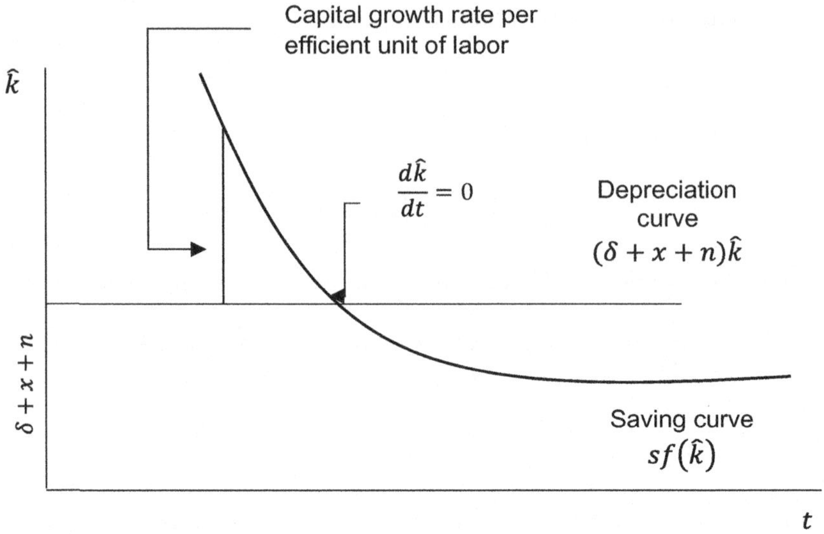

Fig. 3.7 Solow-Swan Neoclassical growth model (*Source* Own elaboration based on Solow-Swan Eq. 7)

Central Banks. This together with the analytical limitations of neoclassical economic theory makes it necessary to revisit the principles of political-economic and scalar action of the State addressed in the previous chapter under the contemporary temporal dimension of the present phase of development or Knowledge Capitalism.

From this perspective, the following two chapters present the study cases of alternative national experiences to neoliberalism, such as the Scandinavian development pathway, specifically Finnish, and the Asian development modality, especially the case of China. Based on strong State actions, these countries have managed to escape economic backwardness or are in the process of doing so, challenging, in the case of China, the hegemony of the United States on the global and virtual scales.

References

Financial Crisis Inquiry Commission. (2011). *Financial Crisis Inquiry Report.* Washington: U.S. Government Printing Office.

Fraser, N. (2017). From Progressive Neoliberalism to Trump—And Beyond. *American Affairs, I, 4*, 46–64.

Freeman, C. & Perez, C. (1988). Structural Crises of Adjustment, Business Cycles and Investment Behavior. In Dosi et al. (Ed.), *Technical Change and Economic Theory* (pp. 38–66). London and New York: Pinter Publishers.

Gramsci, A. (1971). *La política y el Estado moderno. Antología de Il materialismo storico e la filosofia di Benedetto Croce y Note sul Machiavelli, sulla politica e sullo stato moderno.* Barcelona: Ediciones Península.

Gramsci, A. (1999). *Cuadernos de la cárcel.* México: Era, Benemérita Universidad Autónoma de Puebla.

Mandel, E. (1979). *El capitalismo tardío.* México: Era.

Mandel, E. (1986). *Las ondas largas del desarrollo capitalista. La interpretación marxista.* Madrid: Siglo XXI Editores.

Marx, C. (2001). *El Capital. Crítica de la economía política.* México: Fondo de Cultura Económica.

Perez, C. (2004). *Revoluciones tecnológicas y capital financiero. La dinámica de las grandes burbujas financieras y las épocas de bonanza.* México: Siglo XXI.

Rodríguez, J. (2005). *La nueva fase de desarrollo económico y social del capitalismo mundial* (Tesis doctoral). México: Universidad Nacional Autónoma de México.

Sandoval, L. (2008). *Nikolai Dmitrievich Kondratiev. Los ciclos largos de la coyuntura económica.* México: UNAM.

Schumpeter, J. (1997). *Teoría del desenvolvimiento económico: una investigación sobre ganancias, capital, crédito, interés y ciclo económico.* México: Fondo de Cultura Económica.

Schumpeter, J. (2002). *Ciclos económicos. Análisis teórico, histórico y estadístico del proceso capitalista.* Zaragoza: Prensas universitarias de Zaragoza.

CHAPTER 4

Finland: The Innovate State

After the fall of the Berlin Wall, Finland went through a period of economic crisis that lasted during the first years of the nineties. After joining the European Union together with Austria and Sweden, began a boom period that would extend for more than a decade, becoming one of the most competitive nations of the new phase of capitalist development at the dawn of the twenty-first century. There is a wide discussion about Finland from the static equilibrium perspective of neoclassical theory that relates investment in research and development, as well as the building of its innovation system, as endogenous factors that led it to move notably from a forest to a knowledge-based economy.

However, these studies do not take into account that this transition was not automatically but rather went through three key moments to overcome backwardness: first the formation of an industrial bourgeoisie around forest exploitation in the second half of the nineteenth century, second obtaining a relative political autonomy from the Soviet Union to promote an endogenous industrial nucleus around the metal-mechanic and telecommunications branches after WWII and third the undertaking during the nineties of a development modality other than neoliberalism based on a society of innovation through learning. In all of them, the political–economic and spatial action of the State played a fundamental role.

C. M. Sánchez Ramírez, *Knowledge Capitalism and State Theory*, Palgrave Insights into Apocalypse Economics,
https://doi.org/10.1007/978-3-030-71411-6_4

This chapter addresses the Finnish State in Knowledge Capitalism in three sections from the space–time approach developed in the previous two. The first section *Social classes, space, and Historic Bloc* exposes the conformation of social classes and groups and their spatial–economic actions based on the historical look of Alapuro (2019), Tarnaala (2001) and Kirby (2010). The second presents *Social Democracy, cooperatives and education* as Gramscian institutions that worked as tool for ruling classes to build their Hegemony over the subaltern fractions and cement the Historic Bloc around an industrialization project. Finally, the third section *State and innovation society through learning as development pathway* explains the formation of a development modality focused on learning and collaborative labor around the information and telecommunications industry promoted by an Innovate State.

4.1 Social Classes, Space and Historic Bloc

After the independence of Finland from Russian rule in 1917, the biggest social contradictions within the Historic Bloc took place in the south-western region of the country, in places like Tampere, where the largest estates were located as well as the most industrialized areas. Industrial bourgeoisie and landlords were closely related as industrialization process was based mainly on the exploitation of forests, which represents a specific characteristic of Finland not present in other part of Europe.

The industrial bourgeoisie came mainly from nobility social layers that had formed since the territory was under control of the Swedish kingdom. The nobles were landowners who had access to higher education and held key positions in the government administrative bureaucracy. The bureaucratic elite acting as organic intellectuals of the ruling classes promoted an industrialization process from the State, forming an industrial and commercial bourgeois class around the establishment of sawmills, pulp mills and paper factories and removing administrative restrictions to unleash capitalist development. Bureaucracy led the action of the restricted State establishing an institutional structure of the State or State projects through a centralized administrative apparatus that carried out the tasks of territorial consolidation, centralization and economic integration among the different geographical scales of the Finnish territory.

Thus, State allowed steam mills in 1859 and abolished all restrictions on cutting wood from the forest in 1861. Between 1860 and 1877, total saw wood production increased sevenfold, and the number of steam sawmills increased to seventy percent of the total. This way, industrial bourgeoisie consolidated since the eighties of the nineteenth century, through the expansion of the wood industry into large companies that developed new ones around paper and wood pulp production and increasing their class investments by buying glass factories and foundries. The Finnish national bourgeoisie was better able to overcome the crisis of 1873, which forced many foreign businessmen in Finland to close or sell their newly built and equipped sawmills, which ended up in the hands of local capitalists. By 1913, the growth of wood industries (lumber, pulp, paper and other products) was such that they accounted for three-quarters of the total value of Finnish exports.

Small leaseholders or crofters were a medium social class who obtained their main livelihood from farming a minimum of three hectares. This social layer maintained a greater social struggle with the landowners of the southwest of the country, where the land rental system was more widespread and the problems derived from the magnitude of the rents and the longer duration of the contracts than in other regions of the country. However, in the rest of the territory, particularly in the western region the conflict between dominant and subordinate classes was less intense because the farmer pathway tended to predominate. This is, the existence of small farms, which out of more than 221 thousand, only around a thousand exceeded one hundred hectares.

As industrialization based on forest exploitation converges in the same space with agricultural development, the agricultural and industrial working classes frequently exchanged the scope of labor reproduction and jointly faced problems with dominant classes. This situation generated a natural sympathy from the subaltern classes to the social democratic movement that communicated them and facilitated their organization. The deepening of the social imbalance between landowners and agrarian workers in the south of the country led to the social outbreak and civil war between 1917 and 1918. After that, ruling classes yielded an agrarian reform to guarantee the crofters right to claim plots property, as well as the expropriation of public and private lands in order to distribute them to the landless.

The transit from an agrarian country, largely rural, into an industrialized nation is due to the consensus among the ruling classes on the need to keep and reinforce the political autonomy of the State. For this, dominant classes found necessary to maintain social cohesion within the Historic Bloc, in order to face the external threat posed by the emergence of the Soviet Union, as well as the internal risks that a new revolution would imply for their interests. Thus, elites carried out a Passive Revolution based primarily on consensus to weave agreements and alliances among the set of classes and social groups to lead industrialization and national development through Gramscian institutions such as social democracy, cooperativism, as well as education and culture.

4.2 Gramscian Institutions and Hegemony

4.2.1 Social Democracy

Origins of social democracy in Finland began in workers' associations founded in the eighties of nineteenth century, promoted by reformers and supported by textile entrepreneurs inspired in the efforts of Danish and German liberals to foster education and rights to organize and strike among labor force in order to prevent the spread of socialism. Entrepreneurs considered workers organization a way to reduce conflicts and educate them to get their active consensus in capitalist reproduction. Finnish middle-class reformers launched the Labor Party in Helsinki in 1897, and later with the support of trade union groups, they formed the National Social Democratic Party of Finland in 1903.

During October 1905, the general strike that paralyzed Finland in demand of its national independence from Russia together the revolutionary crisis in this last country forced the Tsar to grant the Duchy of Finland full freedom to govern itself. This was an opportunity for Social Democrats to push forward their demands for universal suffrage and unicameral assembly. In 1906, parliamentary reforms included women's suffrage, granting equal voting rights for both men and women. In 1907, amid a social upheaval in the Russian Empire and based on universal suffrage that extended to women and men over 24 years old, the Finnish National Assembly was elected in order to establish an unicameral government. The Social Democrats won 80 out of the 200 available seats, including nine women who along with ten others from other parties were the first elected women as members of a parliament. The Assembly proceeded to enact a long series of highly progressive social laws that did not go into effect due to hostility against the Finnish nationalism of the Russian Empire, from which the country became independent ten years later.

However, parliamentary reform driven by the Social Democrats meant the most radical in Europe and provided Finland with the most democratic social representation system among the whole continent. It was the first country in Europe applying universal and equal suffrage and made Finnish women the first eligible women in history. The number of voters multiplied by ten, and for the first time, 85% of the men voted, who had no representation in the old assembly of the general estates, where only dominant classes: the nobility, the bourgeoisie, the landowners and the clergy were represented. In the same way, women, who until then completely lacked political rights, voted. This leap forward was a profound change in the political life of the country as a way for ruling classes to channel the concerns and aspirations of the subaltern ones.

The Social Democratic Party has maintained a relative preeminence in Parliament over time, meaning a barrier to contain the Communist Party, which ruling classes outlawed from 1929 to 1945. Unlike in Eastern Europe, where the Communists were able to dominate the socialist and peasant parties, in Finland this never happened. Furthermore, the Communists never managed to maintain control of the unions, as the Social Democrats did.

4.2.2 Cooperativism

The impact of industrialization centered in wood processing deepened the spread of capitalism. From 1860 to 1900, timber prices rose three or four times, as well as land prices by over three and a half times particularly in south-western and central Finland, thus accelerating agricultural transition from arable farming to stock raising and dairy farming. Farmer pathway boosted market competition. Capitalist rationality drove landowners seeking accumulation to improve means of production, introducing new equipment and modern production methods. Cooperatives became an instrument for landowners to drive and structure the expanding domestic market as agrarian workers also benefited with increasing wages in logging linked to industrialization. Moreover, cooperatives became spaces for economic and social political organization in which the dominant classes incorporated the subordinate ones through consensus around the management of local development problems that took advantage of the municipal self-government reforms of the early seventies of the nineteenth century.

For the last decade of the nineteenth century, the cooperatives also worked as a resistance movement to the increasing repressive measures of the hardened Russian authorities in 1899. The publication of the February Manifesto by Tsar Nicholas II considerably diminished the autonomy of the Duchy of Finland, abrogated its constitution and began an intense process of Russification. This led to a strong protest movement engineered by Finnish ruling classes and organized around cooperatives and working class movement. Becoming an instrument of Hegemony for dominant classes to keep cohesion within the Historic Bloc to face political threats from abroad and local economic challenges, cooperative dairies, farmers' societies and saving banks controlled by landowners proliferated. In 1910, coöperatives had 87 thousand members governed by wealthy peasants and local officials where agrarian–industrial workers and crofters participated as well, serving as a network that linked peripheral localities with the center of the country and vice versa, strengthening the role of civil society in the full State.

4.2.3 Education and Culture

Education had a central role for conservative dominant classes as the landowning peasants and their church and university intellectuals saw their influence diminish, facing the rise of the industrial and commercial bourgeoisie and their Social Democratic intellectuals in the second half of the nineteenth century. Nationalist movement (Fennomania) meant the Finnicisation of Swedish origin nobility who occupying privileged positions in the State bureaucracy conformed fractions of a new industrial bourgeoisie class. It was not the elimination of the industrial class but the need to replace them with a nationalist bourgeoisie coming from freeholding peasants to fade away Swedish culture influence. In order to expand nationalism and increase its social support, conservative classes demanded the adoption of Finnish as an administrative language and the establishment of public elementary schools in rural districts, as well as the implementation of local governments.

Thus, Finnicisation had a double hegemonic objective within the Historic Bloc: on the one hand to build ties of identity between the dominant and subordinate classes—reducing Swedish cultural dominance—via the Finnish language and the spread of Finnish culture through education in order to get the active consensus of the subalterns to support dominant classes interests, particularly those of the landowners and on the other hand to resist Russian dominance through culture and education as instruments for unity. Nationalist movement also promoted cohesion among working classes through the first mass organization of the Finnish workers known as Temperance movement. Social Democratic Party also disputed Temperance social base to the point that during the general strike of 1905 the popular demands reflected both the most conservative anti-capitalist agenda and the reformist agenda of universal suffrage, meaning a social crossover between Fennomania and a kind of left Fennomania.

The establishment and expansion of public elementary schools thru the basic education law enacted in 1866 provided an additional link—apart from the aforementioned location of the industries in the countryside—to forge the political alliance between agrarian and working classes. Moreover, elementary schools located in every Finnish-speaking town where no student had to travel more than a mile to school let upward social mobility from the peasantry to the clergy and benefited the growing middle class as well. Working class movement adopted the use of culture as an instrument of cohesion among subaltern classes, building halls to carry out cultural and political activities such as theatrical and musical performances and social and athletic events. These cultural centres established throughout the territory in big and small towns and in industrial and commercial areas rose from 47 in 1905 to 940 in 1916, becoming and organizational network to integrate lower classes into civil society and full State while preserving a nationalist perspective from its origins in Finnicisation.

4.3 State and Innovation Society Through Learning as Development Pathway

Under the previous Gramscian institutions, Finnish ruling classes managed to maintain and reproduce their hegemonic capacity toward the rest of the classes and groups within the Historic Bloc around the social convenience of keeping the objective of consolidate the industrialization process under national development premises. The organizational strength of civil society provided a relative political autonomy to the Finnish State to integrate the country into the World Order after WWII under the hegemony of two powers, obtaining advantages for the development of its industrial sectors linked to the driving branches of the Fordist–Keynesian phase of development.

During WWII, Finland and the Soviet Union clashed twice. Mainly as consequence of the Winter War (1939–1940) and the Continuation War (1941–1944), USSR forced Finland to pay large war indemnities consisting exclusively on goods deliveries, financed by foreign loans and partially by internal taxes. The Finnish State paid in eight years and achieved the creation of a modern machinery and metallurgical industry (see Table 4.1), which in 1954 accounted for almost a third of its industrial added value, compared to just a fifth in 1937.

The telecommunications industry also had a substantial development, marking the beginning of what would later become one of the key industries in the Finnish economy. Moreover, taking advantage of the strengthening of its industrial capacity, Finland deepen the trading relationship with the Soviet Union which became an important market for its machinery products exports, surpassing the commercial relationship with its Scandinavian neighbors as well as with Germany and equating with that of Great Britain (see Table 4.2) (Cipolla, 1985).

The same hegemonic capacity within the Historic Bloc allowed the Finnish State to cope in the long term with the fall of the USSR in 1991, as well as the rise of neoliberalism as the preponderant Atlantic development pathway of the new phase of development or Knowledge Capitalism and the torrent of global financial resources that had arouse during the eighties in the U.S., razing the geography of the Fordist–Keynesian Welfare State in other countries. Although in Finland a set

Table 4.1 Finnish indemnities to the Soviet Union after World War II

	Millions of dollars (1938 prices)	*Percentage*
Newly built ships	66.0	72
Ships of the 1944 merchant fleet	14.0	
Machinery and other equipment	70.7	
Telecommunications materials	12.9	
Products of paper and pulp	34.9	28
Wood and wood products	28.0	
Total	226.5	100

Source Cipolla (1985)

Table 4.2 Distribution of Finnish foreign trade (export–import percentage) by selected countries 1921–1969

	1921–1925		*1936–1938*		*1955–1958*		*1968–1969*	
	Exp.	Imp.	Exp.	Imp.	Exp.	Imp.	Exp.	Imp.
Great Britain	38	19	40	18	23	17	20	16
Germany	10	32	17	20	10	16	10	16
USSR	**4**	**2**	**0.5**	**1.5**	**17**	**16**	**15**	**15**
Sweden-Denmark	11	12	10	20	7	11	16	19

Source Cipolla (1985)

of financial market deregulation measures carried out since the eighties, the State kept the legal framework for banking supervision unchanged until the dissolution of the Soviet Union. Honkapohja et al. (2009) estimated that the instant removal of 15% of Finnish foreign trade could account for around three percentage points of the total decline of almost seven percent in Finnish real GDP in 1991. This economic crisis meant an increase in public debt from 12 to 60% of GDP in the period of 1990–1995, as well as unemployment increase from three to 18% among the same years (Kiander, 2009).

The reaction to the crisis was not the evaporation of the State, but the absorption of social interest from the hegemonic capacity of the Historic Bloc to undertake a national development pathway different from neoliberalism but under the structural economic determinants of the new phase of development. Social Democrats promoted this process during the sixties through scientific organizations that reflected the interests of civil society from the scope of its actions in the economic sphere. In this way, a fundamental achievement of National Fund for Research and Development (SITRA) established in 1967 was the evaluation report of the impact of technological knowledge on economic growth presented in 1976, which had a great influence on the discussion of technological industrial policy in the midst of an atmosphere of international recession.

SITRA's publication coincided with the early years of the microprocessor technological revolution that had begun to attract international attention and represented the starting point of the series of efforts to focus the political–scientific discussion around the valuation of knowledge and technology as an essential instrument for decision–making within the Finnish Parliament to promote economic growth. Later, at the end of the seventies and during the eighties, a set of committees identified the need to design a national technological industrial policy and pushed actions to achieve this objective.

The year before the economic crisis of 1991, the Council for Science and Technology Policy outlined guidelines to pursue the goal of turning Finland into a society of innovation through learning. Later in mid-nineties, Finland set the objective to become one of the leading information societies not only in Europe but also throughout the world. The Council defined an information society as one in which the information and mass media industries are the main business sector, where the entire population has access to information services as well as the skills to use them and in which processes and the structure of business and the public sector have been developed based on information technologies.

At the same time, the Finnish Parliament approved a working group on technological studies linked to the Finnish Technical Research Center in 1995, whose objective was to prepare a proposal for technological evaluation that would serve as an instrument for Parliament's decision—making on issues related to the impact of technological knowledge on society and economic growth. Using the German Bundestag Office for Technology Assessment as a model, the working group recommended the establishment of a technology assessment subcommittee under the Committee for the Future of Parliament. Four years later, it presented the first evaluations of the impact of technology on Finnish economy, addressing the issues of biotechnology, information and communication technologies in the Finnish education system and gerontechnology.

Thus, during nineties Social Democrats configured a set of scientific–political organizations to build a national consensus around science and technology as the highest priorities for industrial policy to take Finland toward a society of innovation through learning without opposition from other political parties. State, telecommunications enterprises and educational and research institutions had an economic fundamental role in driving this pathway involving the entire population to contribute to the implementation and creation of new technologies to keep economic competitiveness and social welfare.

Cooperatives became the instrument to include subaltern classes in the innovation society, mainly because they share basic principles with Toyotism as labor organization and management method toward the cognitive and creative workforce valorization from multidisciplinary teamwork. The increase in unemployment resulted from the financial economic crisis of 1991 meant the rise of the establishment of new worker cooperatives from a renewed perspective. There were less than 20 worker cooperatives in 1993, increasing to 500 by 2000. Meanwhile, a third of the total related to knowledge valorization, focusing in information technologies and telecommunications, consulting, executive training and architecture sectors (Troberg, 2000).

These knowledge cooperatives established as a dynamic network of knowledge workers with a horizontal democratic decision-making structure and a creative and collaborative organizational culture, sharing values of equity, cooperation and solidarity among its members. Large companies began to subcontract knowledge cooperatives that brought together a set of experts in different disciplines to carry out specific tasks based on knowledge, having telecommunications in general and the Internet in specific as a platform for development and sharing of knowledge, promoting rise of teleworking (Troberg, 2000).

To accomplish the need for capitalist reproduction via teleworking between large companies and knowledge cooperatives, telecommunications companies take-off implied the continued expansion of the geographical coverage of Internet access in most of the country's households (see Fig. 4.1). In 2017, Finland already had the third fastest average

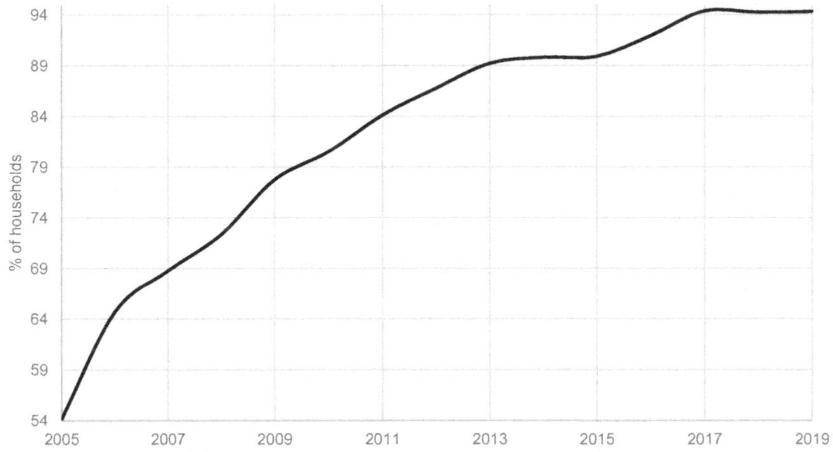

Fig. 4.1 Finland, percentage of households with Internet access (*Source* Own elaboration with OECD data)

mobile network connection speed in Europe behind Great Britain and Germany at 21.6 Mbps on laptops, tablets and smartphones (Akamai, 2017). Furthermore, the State has projected the strengthening of the country's connectivity by 2025 from the deployment of mobile and fiber optic networks to improve connectivity at all geographical scales of the country and guarantee Internet connection in all households at a 100 Mbit/s minimum speed with the possibility of scaling to 1 gigabyte per second. This upgrade of the telecommunications infrastructure will allow the development of artificial intelligence and the Internet of Things, as well as the acceleration of industrial robotizing and automation (Finland Ministry of Transport and Communications, 2018).

In addition to the improving of the telecommunications infrastructure, another fundamental action of the State to guarantee favorable conditions to deploy its development pathway in the new phase of capitalism is the continuous strengthening of education system as a necessary condition for economic development. Education and culture were already fundamental instruments for ruling classes to project their Hegemony to the subaltern ones as described earlier, and since 1921, school attendance was legislated as a basic and mandatory principle for all children between 7 and 12 years old.

Dutta, Lanvin, and Paua (2004) suggest that Finland began to strength its educational system between the sixties and seventies of the twentieth century. During this period, basic education consolidated as compulsory, comprising nine years, from seven to 16. In coincidence with the previous authors, Castells and Himanen (2002) point out that Finnish university system foundation strengthened in 1960 and their financial situation improved. Until then, Finland had full universities in only two cities. Nevertheless, through the Council for Science Policy, 20 high-quality, free, public universities were developed by 1970 in ten cities. Since then onwards, Finland has made a continuous expenditure on education of at least four percent of its gross domestic product (see Fig. 4.2).

As a result, the percentage of the labor force employed with higher education has been growing almost steadily since 1987, representing 37% in 2017 (see Fig. 4.3). Between 2000 and 2008, electronic and telecommunications technologies and science and education as driving sectors of Knowledge Capitalism concentrated an average of 22% of population with higher education. Meanwhile, automotive, metal-mechanic and petrochemical, as Fordist–Keynesian driving industries concentrated 13% in average of this population. Nevertheless, public administration and health

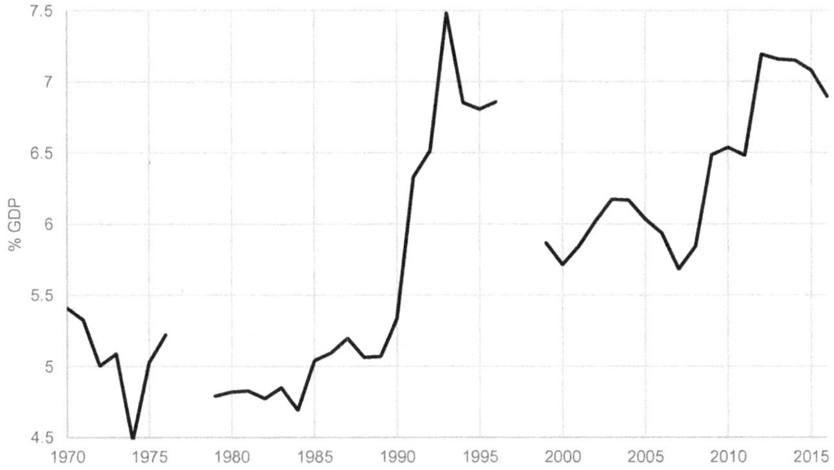

Fig. 4.2 Finland public expenditure on education as percentage of GDP (*Source* Own elaboration with World Bank data)

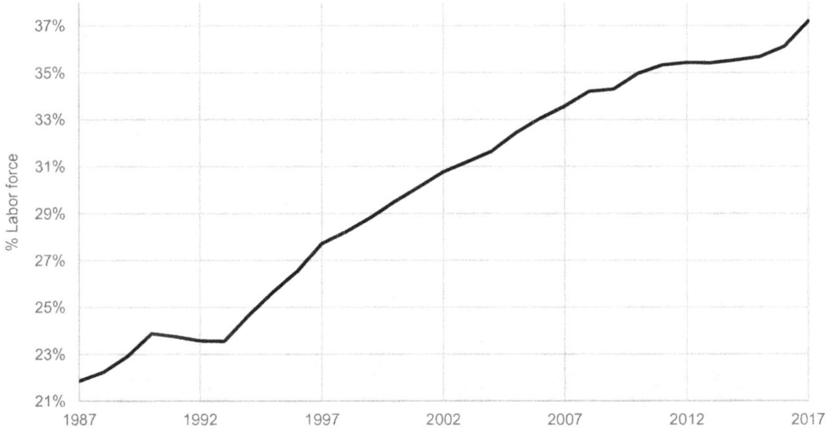

Fig. 4.3 Finland percentage of labor force employed with higher education (*Source* Own elaboration with Statistics Finland data)

services absorbed 27%, and commerce and financial services 25%, both in average (see Fig. 4.4).

Based on the strength of the education system and the deployment of scientific organizations to boost strategic industrial branches, there was an increasing expenditure in national research and development (R&D) from the eighties that tended to sharp during the nineties. This placed Finland progressively above the United States and South Korea on this indicator, as well as above the average of the OECD countries and the European Union. However, R&D expenditure growth rate began to show signs of stagnation after the Dot-Com bubble burst in 2001, becoming a declining trend after the productive financial crisis of 2008, placing the

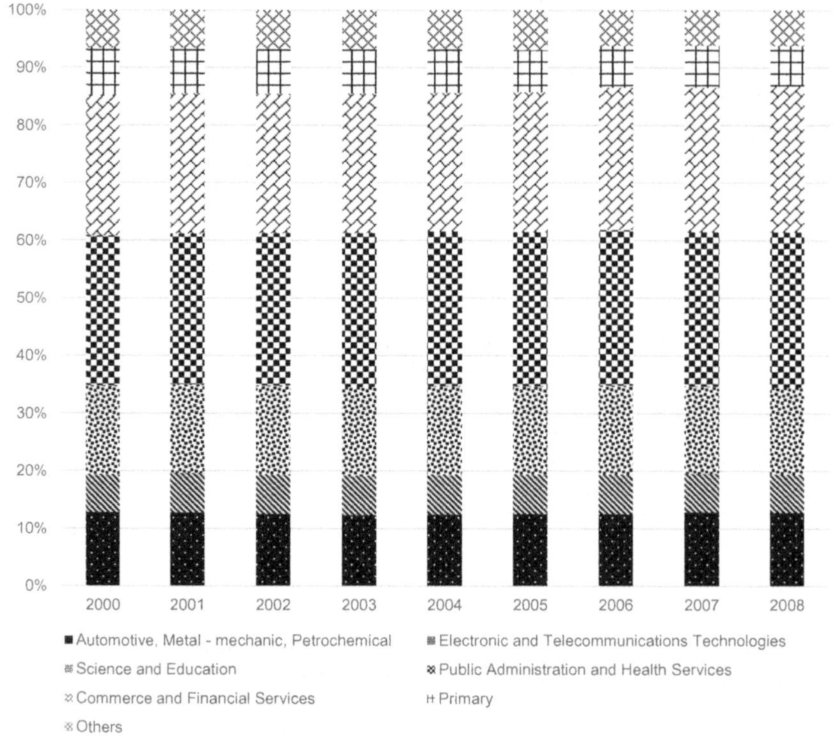

Fig. 4.4 Finland employed population with higher education by industry in 2000–2008 (*Source* Own elaboration with Statistics Finland data)

country in recent years below the United States although still above the E.U. and OECD averages (see Fig. 4.5). Especially, the entrepreneurial scope shows this slowdown turning point in R&D expenditure after housing bubble burst (see Fig. 4.6).

From a first impulse from the State during the seventies, enterprises began a growing trend in R&D expenditure during subsequent decades, which took shape in the continuous increase in the percentage of national patents applied in Finland compared to foreign applications, since Finnish´s represented practically ninety percent of the total since 1998 (see Fig. 4.7).

However, the productive financial crisis of 2008, in addition to weakening enterprises spending on R&D, also had a negative impact on the trend of the electric and electronics industrial production as an important component of the driving industries in Knowledge Capitalism. During the nineties, the electrical and electronic industrial production growth rate had significant increases above the rest of the industrial branches as well as relative modest increases during the first decade of this century, showing a decline below the rest of the industrial sectors after 2008 (see Fig. 4.8).

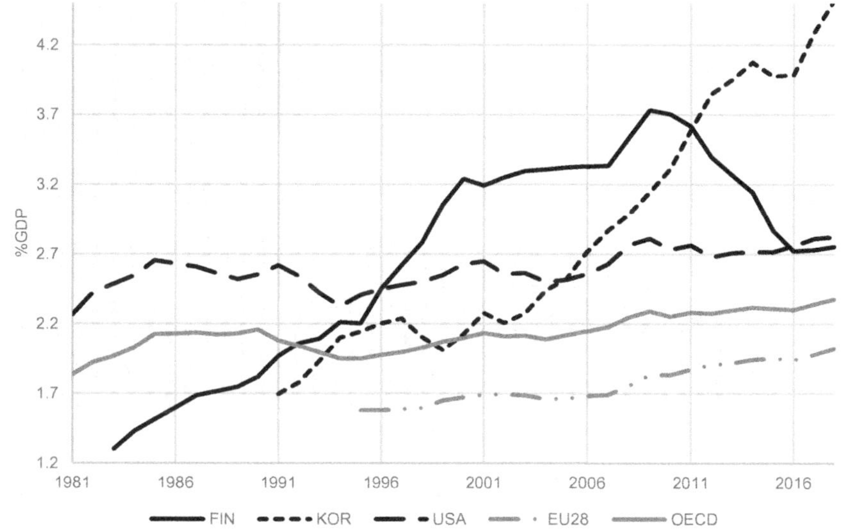

Fig. 4.5 R&D expenditure as percentage of GDP, selected countries and regions (*Source* Own elaboration with OECD data)

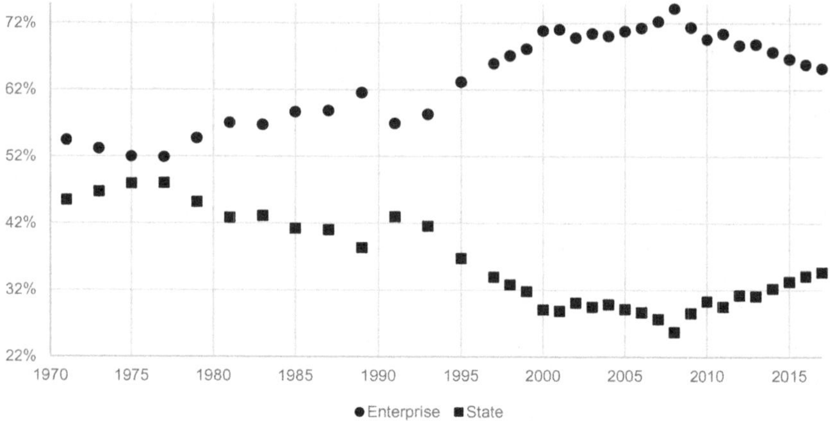

Fig. 4.6 Finnish state and enterprise R&D percentage expenditures (*Source* Own elaboration with Statistics Finland data)

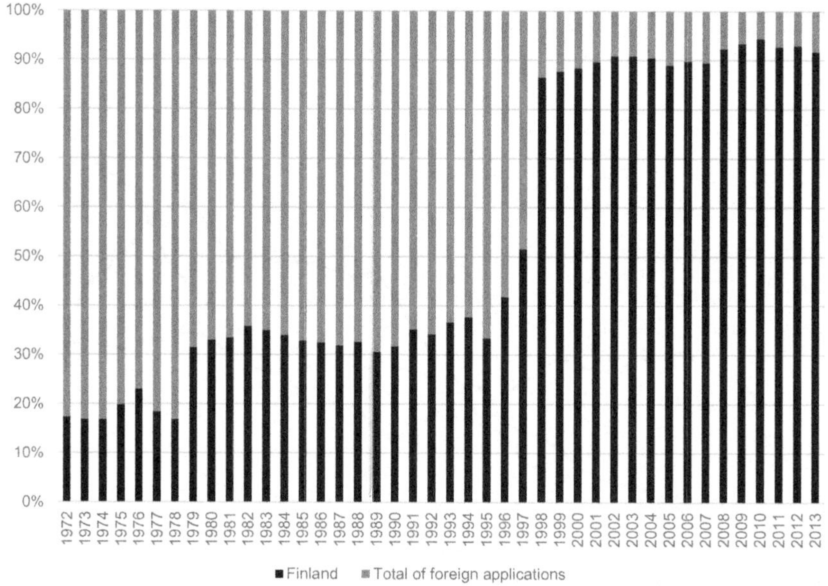

Fig. 4.7 Percentage of applied patents in Finland by residence of applicants (*Source* Own elaboration with Statistics Finland data)

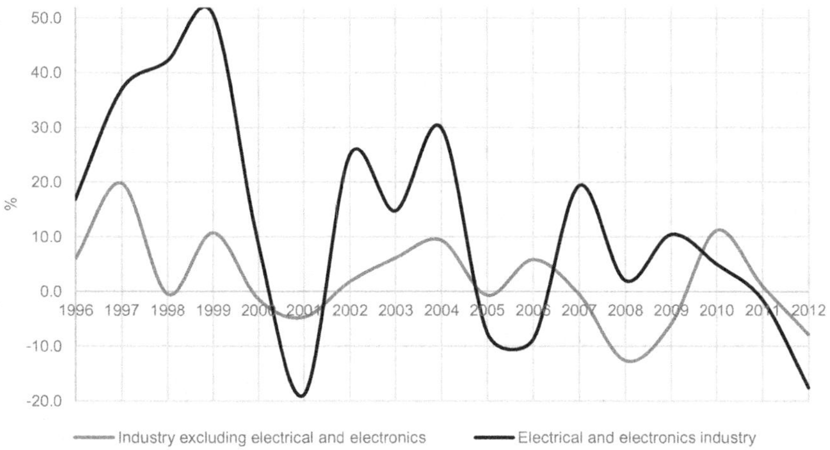

Fig. 4.8 Finland industrial output growth rate (*Source* Own elaboration with Statistics Finland data)

Finland overcame economic backwardness undertaking a development pathway driven by an Innovate State resulting from a strong hegemonic capacity of the ruling classes within the Historic Bloc. The social convenience of the maximum economic expansion of the ruling classes spread to the rest of classes through social democracy, cooperativism and education and culture as instruments of Hegemony and incorporation of the socio-economic interests of society within the Historic Bloc. These hegemonic instruments or Gramscian institutions allowed a broad development of civil society easing consensus around undertaking a development pathway based on the national agreement of a society of innovation through learning under the economic–structural basement of the new phase of development or Knowledge Capitalism.

To achieve this political–economic objective of civil society, the State drove an industrial development policy to promote electronics and telecommunications technologies industrial branches, based on the technological revolution of the microprocessor and software development and closely linked to the labor cognitive and creative valorization under the foundation of social inclusion and carried out through cooperatives. Therefore, these characteristics distinguish the Finnish State development experience from neoliberal modalities in Western Europe. The Innovate

Finnish State is then understand as the result of a renewed democratic social consensus under the national agreement of a society of innovation and learning, which promotes a flexible production based on creativity and knowledge compatible with social equality.

The Innovate State successfully overcame the financial economic crisis of 1991, derived from the fall of the Soviet Union and the rise of neoliberalism, increasing the differential GDP per capita growth rate compared to the average of the European Union during nineties and until 2007. Nevertheless, the crisis of 2008 characterized by the growing decoupling between the spheres of productive and financial capitals on a global scale has imposed a new challenge for consensus within the Historic Bloc around a society of innovation and social inclusion seen thru the fall of GDP per capita growth rate below the average of the E.U. (see Fig. 4.9).

Decoupling between the spheres of capital as an expression of decline of neoliberalism as an Atlantic-hegemonic development pathway and the rise of the Chinese competitive State highlight a confrontation between antagonistic development modalities on a global scale. Having this supranational scenario, inside Finland the Social Democratic Party has lost specific weight in recent elections, society views cooperatives less as spaces

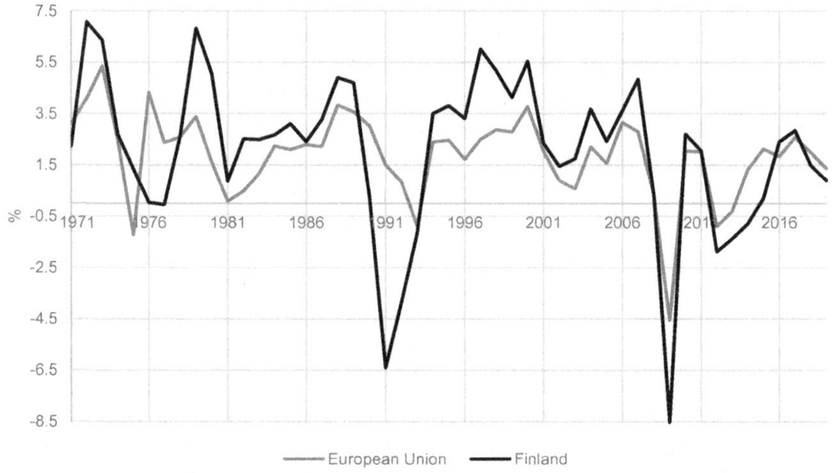

Fig. 4.9 Finland and European Union GDP per capita growth rate (*Source* Own elaboration with World Bank data)

for solving the socio-economic conflict, and the trend of State expenditure on public education is decreasing, thus posing a new challenge to the Innovate State as a Nordic emblematic development pathway that shows signs of neoliberalization and exhaustion of the Gramscian institutions that cement the whole of civil society within the Historic Bloc.

References

Alapuro, R. (2019). *State and revolution in Finland*. Amsterdam and Leiden: Brill.

Akamai. (2017). *Akamai's State of the Internet. Q1 2017 report* (Volume 10, Number 1). Retrieved from https://www.akamai.com/fr/fr/multimedia/documents/state-of-the-internet/q1-2017-state-of-the-internet-connectivity-report.pdf.

Castells, M., & Himanen, P. (2002). *The information society and the welfare state: The Finnish model*. New York: Oxford University Press.

Cipolla, C. (Ed). (1985). *Historia económica de Europa. Economías contemporáneas. Segunda parte*. Barcelona: Ariel.

Dutta, S., Lanvin, B., & Paua, F. (Eds.). (2004). *The global information technology report 2003–2004: Towards and equitable information society (GITR)*. New York: Oxford University Press.

Finland Ministry of Transport and Communications. (2018). *Digital infrastructure strategy: Turning Finland into the world leader in communications networks*. Retrieved from https://www.lvm.fi/en/-/digital-infrastructure-strategy-turning-finland-into-the-world-leader-in-communications-networks-985076.

Honkapohja, S., Koskela, E., Leibfritz, W., & Uusitalo, R. (2009). *Economic prosperity recaptured: The Finnish path from crisis to rapid growth*. Cambridge: The MIT Press.

Kiander, J. (April, 2009). The great depression of Finland 1990–1993: Causes and consequences. In P. O'Connell (Presidency), *The Labour market in recession*. Conference in Economic and Social Research Institute Policy Conference 2009, Dublin, Ireland.

Kirby, D. (2010). *Historia de Finlandia*. Madrid: Akal.

Tarnaala, E. (2001). La Guerra civil en Finlandia y la cuestión agraria en Europa en los inicios del siglo XX. *Revista Opera, 1*(1), 283–299.

Troberg, E. (2000). Knowledge intensive business sector and the cooperative form: A study of Finnish knowledge intensive cooperatives. *Journal of Rural Cooperation, 28*(2), 161–174.

CHAPTER 5

China: The Visible Hand of the State

The Chinese pathway in the new phase of development is an important reference in the understanding of the role of the State in Knowledge Capitalism. China's spectacular economic performance since 1976 drove it just over four decades later as a new great power with global reach, contesting the United States hegemony and becoming its largest creditor. Inwards, the Asian giant strengths and consolidates its domestic market, meanwhile outwards looks forward to build a new International System of States Hegemony.

The role of the State in China is a deep discussion topic, considering its particular development pathway in which a process of different speeds was unleashed at different territorial scales, from statist to capitalism guided by the visible hand of the State. The construction of its specific development modality put aside the political thought of Marxism–Leninism under the Maoist interpretation of the Chinese bureaucracy in power, and its substitution by pragmatism from the rising reformist bureaucratic faction with Deng Xiaoping at the forefront.

A first sight to the People's Republic of China industrial development long-term trajectory shows the following stages: A first period of Communist reconstruction and growth from 1949 to 1957 that includes the First Five-Year Plan (1953–1957), a second period or Great Leap Forward development strategy from 1958 to 1961, a third period of economic

C. M. Sánchez Ramírez, *Knowledge Capitalism and State Theory*, Palgrave Insights into Apocalypse Economics,
https://doi.org/10.1007/978-3-030-71411-6_5

recovery from 1962 to 1965 and a fourth period that spans from the Cultural Revolution that began in 1966 to the death of Mao Tse-Tung in 1976, and the beginning of a broad transition process in China promoted by Deng Xiaoping, distinguished by wide reforms in the fields of agriculture, industry, science and technology as well as defense. This chapter addresses Chinese transition between fourth and fifth periods, from a State-planned economy to a mercantile capitalist one on the way to becoming a hegemonic power in the new phase of development.

From this perspective, the first section explains the Third Front program within the Cultural Revolution period as the last Chinese industrialization attempt under Mao leadership and *mass line* development pathway or politics in command. The Third Front analysis meets three objectives. To provide elements to understand the exhaustion of mass line development pathway during statist period, trace the origin of electronic State-owned enterprises as a driving branch of Knowledge Capitalism and to show Maoist State spatial selectivity to develop north China based on ideological–military premises.

The second section outlines the Chinese Historic Bloc reconfiguration process during the transition stage begun in 1976 through the ideological dispute between conservatives and reformists fractions of the Chinese Communist Party. This reconfiguration included intellectuals, subaltern classes and mainly the Chinese bourgeoisie economic interests settled outside the continental territory or Great China meaning a Passive Revolution in order to build a new Hegemony around pragmatism and economy in command as development pathway. Finally, the last section discusses the Chinese Competitive State economic–spatial strategies from agriculture, industry and commerce reforms that let the country to insert itself in the low and medium value chains of global division of labor, to the increasing research and development investment to climb progressively to the high cognitive value-added chains.

Contrasting with the incipient exhaustion of the Finnish Innovate State, and declining neoliberalism, the rise of the visible hand of the Chinese State in the global stage seems to consolidate through the overseas projection of its own development pathway. Belt and Road Initiative and a massive investment in disruptive edge technologies as artificial intelligence, quantum computing and 5G telecommunication networks put China ahead toward a post-COVID-19 new World Order.

5.1 The Third Front: Limits of Mass Line as a Chinese Development Pathway During Cultural Revolution

For the Chinese Communist Party (CCP), the creation of a unified State had industrialization as one of the economic pillars for national development. Nevertheless, it did not mean the need to follow economic strategies of other countries with different and distant cultural traditions. The answer to this problem should come from national premises. Thus, the solution built by Mao Tse-Tung was the mass line strategy applied during revolution, the latter understood not only as a process of social, economic and political emancipation, but as a transforming cultural phenomenon of the individual, that merge him with the masses, that socializes him, producing a "new man." This Maoist understand of the revolutionary struggle was transferred to the superstructural sphere of Chinese society and used as a methodology of direction and development pathway.

> In all the practical work of our Party, all correct leadership is necessarily based on the principle: "from the masses, to the masses". This means collecting the ideas (dispersed and not systematic) of the masses and synthesizing them (transforming them, through study, into synthesized and systematized ideas) and then taking them to the masses, disseminating them and explaining them, so that the masses make them their own, persevere in them and translate them into action, and verify in the action of the masses the correctness of those ideas. Then, it is necessary to collect and synthesize the ideas of the masses and bring them to the masses to persist in them, and so on indefinitely, so that the ideas become fairer, more alive and richer in content. Such is the Marxist theory of knowledge. (Tse-Tung, 1972)

This Maoist interpretation of Marxist theory was present in the debates of society and the Chinese bureaucracy in power since the beginning of the People's Republic, also permeating economic policy since the Great Leap Forward, which meant a drop in real GDP growth bigger than 27% points in 1961 (see Fig. 5.1). Later, during Cultural Revolution,[1] mass line evidenced again its inability to industrialize the country,

[1] During the period of the Cultural Revolution, "... the Red Guards turned to destructive activities that led to a brutal reign of terror, breaking into the homes of wealthy

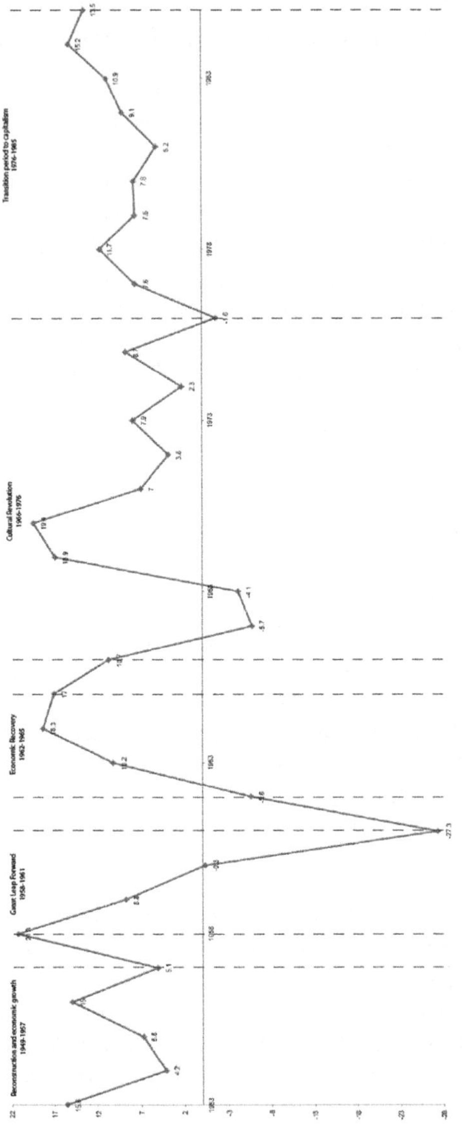

Fig. 5.1 China GDP real growth rate 1953–1985 (*Source* Own elaboration with World Bank data)

particularly during the period known as the Third Front, described by Naughton (1988) on whom this section data bases on, as an extensive, hasty, militarized and with a high pattern of territorial dispersion investment program, that accelerated the subsequent ideological crisis within the Chinese bureaucracy.

Cultural Revolution period juxtaposes with that of United States aggression against Vietnam. In this context, and driven by the suspicion of an invasion of Chinese territory, the State promoted a strategy of spatial selectivity, characterized by massive investment in the military and industrial development of remote provinces in the northwest and southwest of China (see Fig. 5.2), in order to build self-sufficient bases for defense in mountainous areas with difficult access. State also deployed new railway tracks through the mountains to link the new weapon and machinery industries, iron mines, steel mills and hydroelectric power plants. This massive investment within China was the Third Front, originally proposed as a military strategy between 1965 and 1971 to reduce Chinese vulnerability to a foreign invasion, due to industrial concentration in some coastal regions of the country. At the same time, the term refers to the geographical area in which the program took place, carried out in two phases.

The first phase of the Third Front focused on the southwestern provinces: Sichuan, Yunnan and Guizhou in order to create a complete industrial structure, beginning with mining–energy production and culminating with the assembly of sophisticated machinery, including military equipment, plans that required the priority construction of a rail transport network. The second phase began in 1969 concentrated in the area of intersection between Hubei, Henan and Shaanxi, extending toward the west of Hunan and toward the east of Sichuan and Guizhou. In the same way, the objective was to create an industrial structure, centered on a railway network, hydroelectric power plants and especially machine building (highlighting the automobile plant in Shiyan, northwest of Hubei), including the military one.

families, intellectuals and officials, destroying books and manuscripts, humiliating, beating and even murdering the inhabitants, and continually claiming to be carrying out the revolutionary attack against the 'Four Old Men': old ideas, old culture, old rights, old habits. These young students, boys and girls alike, whose ages ranged from nine to eighteen, roamed the streets with their red bands on their arms, harassing and imparting their own moral justice to anyone who showed the slightest hint of foreigners or foreigners intellectualism" (Fairbank & Goldman, 2006).

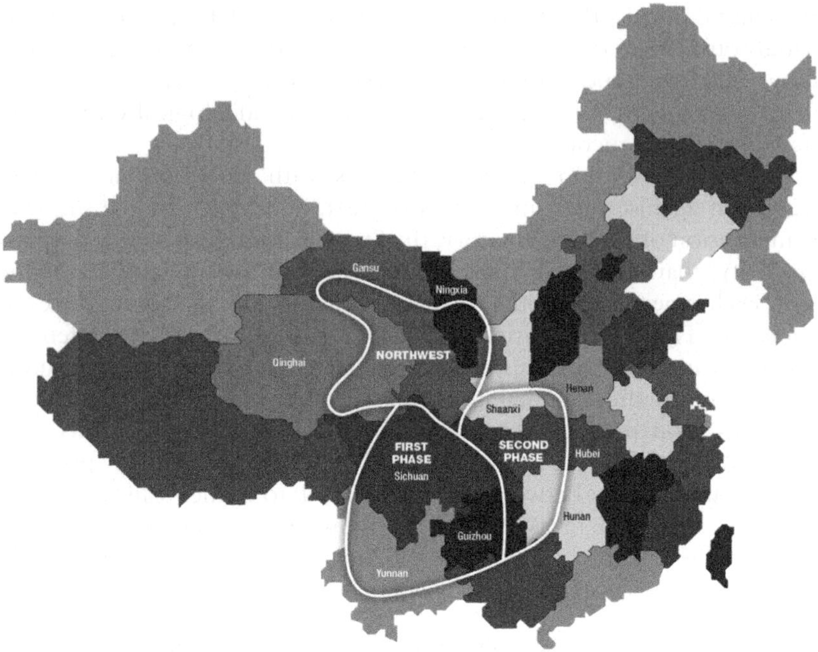

Fig. 5.2 Chinese Third Front area The Third Front area included the provinces of Sichuan, Yunnan, Guizhou, Gansu, Qinghai and Ningxia, a part of Shaanxi (south of the Qinling Mountains) and to the west, the mountainous areas of Henan, Hubei and Hunan. The line that demarcates regions with altitudes above 500 meters encloses the Third Front. Within the circumference are lowland regions, especially the Sichuan Basin and the Han River Valley surrounded and protected by a mountainous region (*Source* Author's own creation based on Naughton (1988))

The construction period of the Third Front finished in 1971. Many projects were suspended or completed between 1972 and 1973 and the construction brigades transferred to other projects in eastern China as well as many of the temporary workers returned to their communities of origin. Within the Third Front, priorities reassigned and workers transferred to projects close to completion, while other projects with little chance of immediate completion were suspended. This change in the orientation of Chinese national policy was due to the beginning of

Table 5.1 Investment in the Chinese Third Front as a proportion of national investment

Period	*Percentage (%)*
1963–1965	38.2
Third Five-Year Plan (1966–1970)	52.7
Fourth Five-Year Plan (1971–1975)	41.1

Source Naughton (1988)

the rapprochement with the United States, in response to the growing hostility of the USSR. In addition, decision accelerated because of the fall and death of General Lin Biao,[2] Vice Chairman of Chairman Mao in September 1971, as the main precursor of Cultural Revolution and the Third Front, but contrary to Mao's thesis in favor of a rapprochement with the United States. Under these conditions, the Third Front lost its main driver, apart from Mao, combined with the reduction of Chinese isolation that diminished hostile threats in the short term.

The magnitude of the Third Front political–military importance performs in economic terms through the program investment proportion compared to national investment in the framework of the Five-Year Plans as shown in Table 5.1. Areas belonging to the Third Front had 37.4% of the industrial fixed capital in 1977, as well as 40% of the fixed capital of the First Ministry of Machinery Construction system around 1981.

Despite the fact that in military terms, the strategy of the Third Front lost validity in the face of the exhaustion of the Fordist–Keynesian phase of development and in the process of emergence of Knowledge Capitalism in the United States during the first half of the seventies, in the economic scope the Third Front expresses ambivalent results. On the one hand, the large amount of resources aimed at the construction of military industrial complexes in inaccessible areas of the Chinese territory meant an extremely costly effort. On the other hand, the Third Front's strategy made it possible to advance rapidly in the idea of the necessary industrial development in the interior areas of the country, carrying out actions that otherwise would have implied more time.

[2] During the climax of the Cultural Revolution, at the 9th Congress of the Chinese People's Party in April 1969, new party statutes were presented, stipulating that General Lin Biao, in his capacity as Vice Chairman of Chairman Mao, was "the closest comrade in arms and successor to Comrade Mao Tse – Tung" (Fairbank & Goldman, 2006).

These actions included the creation of a rail network connecting previously isolated areas of China, the exploitation of ferrous and non-ferrous mineral resources, and the deploy of some reasonably efficient manufacturing companies. Table 5.2 shows the main transport indicators from 1949 to 1980. An important increase in the infrastructure of land, river and air transport stands out, as well as the volume of merchandise transported by these means between 1957 (eight years before of the beginning of the Third Front) and 1977 (six years after its term). Moreover, because of the withdrawal of Soviet assistance, most of the Third Front's projects relied on its own technical capabilities, sometimes complemented by the importation of key technologies. In many cases, Chinese technicians made breakthroughs in problem solving, equipping Chinese industry with indispensable parts for their machinery.

Since many industrial sectors were included in the development of the Third Front under the strategy of producing machinery for industrial and military purposes, the development of this machinery could

Table 5.2 China transport indicators 1949–1980

Type of transport	*1949*	*1952*	*1957*	*1977*	*1978*	*1979*	*1980*
Railroad lines (thousands km)	22.0	24.5	29.9	49.5	50.4	51.5	na
Roads (thousands km)	80.7	126.7	254.6	855.6	890.0	na	na
Waterways (thousands km)	73.6	95.0	144.1	137.4	136.0	na	na
Civil aviation lines (thousands km)	11.4	13.1	26.4	132.1	148.9	160.0	na
Total volume of transported goods (Billions of metric tons per km)							
By rail	25.5	76.2	181.0	795.8	980.6	1098.7	1202.6
By road	18.4	60.2	134.6	455.7	533.3	558.8	571.7
By waterways	0.8	1.4	4.8	25.1	23.4	26.8	76.4
By air transport	0.02	na	0.01	0.08	0.10	0.12	0.14
Oil and gas transported by pipeline	–	–	–	38.7	41.9	47.6	49.1
Freight traffic of the main ports (millions of metric tons)	8.72	14.40	37.27	159.69	198.34	212.57	217.31

Source Banco Exterior de España (1986)

play an important role in the development process due to its linkage with other production sectors, building different productive chains from these simple and extended reproduction schemes.[3] However, due to the installation of industrial complexes motivated by political–military reasons in isolated regions of the country, this industrialization strategy did not achieve its full potential, representing one of the great failures of the mass line comparable to the Great Leap Forward.

In the first half of the eighties of the twentieth century, the reconfigured national development strategy discussed in the next sections divided the country into three industrial levels. The first priority level was for coastal areas, especially through the importing of advanced technology, while medium technologies gradually transferred to the second industrial level in the interior of the country toward centrally located industrial cities. The third level with the lowest priority was the Third Front area. This strategy included in the Five-Year Plans of the time, represented an implicit recognition that most of the investments in technology and machinery construction in the Third Front areas were not useful as a basis for further development. Thus, State implemented plans for the gradual management of the existing Third Front factories. Some of them have maintained priority investment flows such as the No. 2 Car plant in Hubei, which carried out an expansion toward the production of heavy vehicles in 1985.

In this scheme of rescuing the few factories with the possibility of getting ahead, the electronics and military industry companies built during the Third Front stand out, having some of the most advanced technologies in China. The Ministry of Electronics reorganized the Zhenhua Electronics Corporation from its factories in Guizhou, in order to turn its production around and increasingly orient it toward civil and international production. This Corporation began in 1981 to establish projects (generally joint ventures with Chinese and foreign firms) in Chinese coastal cities and in Special Economic Zones (SEZs) dedicated to production and export as well as the import and dissemination of technical information and market. By 1987, military and electronic firms had

[3] Developed by Marx in chapters XX and XXI of Volume II of *Das Kapital*, simple reproduction refers to modern technology in industrial machinery required in all industrial sectors: the machinery sector supplies the other sectors of the industry. Meanwhile extended reproduction refers to complex machine building generating strong demand for goods and services from a wide range of industries.

created more than a thousand such companies in Sichuan, Shaanxi and Guizhou, mainly in the SEZs. In addition to facilitating the movement of technology and workforce, these facilities gradually transfer production to the coastal areas.

5.2 Reconfiguring the Chinese Historic Bloc Under a New Hegemony: The Economy in Command

The starting point of the transition period in China from a State economy to a mercantile capitalist one was the ideological confrontation within Chinese bureaucracy between conservatives and reformists, which took place at the end of Cultural Revolution meaning changes in the internal configuration of the Chinese Historic Bloc. Groups of intellectuals within the CCP previously persecuted emerged at the end of Cultural Revolution and death of Mao Tse-Tung in 1976 joining high-level veteran moderate leaders as Deng Xiaoping. This group clashed against the ultra-leftists belonging to the sphere of political influence of the Gang of Four[4] for control of the Party.

The focus of the struggle for power between these two antagonistic groups centered in the ideological sphere, in the dialectic of theory and practice. This is a double interpretation of the Marxist theory of knowledge, understood from the Maoist perspective of the masses, in which the epistemological postulate "practice is the criterion for verifying truth" acquires a renewed meaning for rising moderate leaders, whose counterpart is Mao's insistence in his later years to give theory a decisive

[4] The Gang of Four were a group of Chinese Communist Party leaders accused of the excesses committed during the Cultural Revolution. The group consisted of Jiang Qing, Mao's wife, who was in charge of the cultural apparatus of the State, as well as three radical intellectuals, leaders of the CCP in Shanghai, Zhang Chunqiao, Yao Wenyuan and Wang Hongwen. In this group is included Lin Biao, military strategist and forerunner of the Cultural Revolution and the Third Front, who compiled all the quotes from Chairman Mao in the Little Red Book. The Gang launched a series of theses on alleged "new mutations" in class relations in the period of socialism. By "new mutations" they meant that veteran cadres had become "leaders following the capitalist path," that veteran workers had become "beneficiaries of vested interests," that young workers were "even worse," that poor peasants and lower-middle peasants were "lagged behind ideologically" from the socialist revolution and, in short, that intellectuals were "stinky people number nine" (after the eight types of class enemies: landlords, rich peasants, counterrevolutionaries, rightist noxious elements, renegades, secret agents of the enemy and inveterate leaders followers of the capitalist pathway) (Bettelheim, Rossanda & Karol, 1978).

role. This renewed view of the Marxist theory of knowledge postulates that our concrete representations even when they come to already known phenomena deepen from the new practical data in new historical conditions, thus gaining in accuracy and transforming in a substantial way, and that practical activity is the safest and only way to verify the truth or falsity of the theory. This perspective gained ground within the CCP to "integrate universal principles of Marxism–Leninism–Maoism in the concrete practice of socialist modernization and develop them under the new historical conditions" (Nee & Mozingo, 1989).

The sociological field interpreted this epistemological principle on practice as the criterion of truth that inspires decisions and actions assuming that each sphere of social life has its own characteristics and governs itself by objective laws. Political leadership can and should create the structure and general conditions favorable to the operation of these laws without suffering serious consequences, that is, a reinterpretation of the principle of "politics in command" (Nee & Mozingo, 1989). The foregoing fully coincides with the need for the political action of the restricted State or political society in backward countries as one of the foundations of the space–time relativity of the State discussed in Chapter 2. This is the State deployment of a structural economic–spatial strategy in order to create favorable conditions for capitalist reproduction under the structural requirements of a historical time dimension of capitalism.

One of the intellectual theorists who rejoined the political–ideological discussion after the Cultural Revolution developing elements to reinterpret "politics in command" under the broader framework of practice as a source of truth was Hu Chiao-mu, president of the newly created Academy of Social Sciences, member of the Party Secretariat and the Political Bureau in 1980 and 1982, respectively. In an article published in the Peking Review, based on a speech at a meeting of the State Council in July 1978, entitled "Observing economic laws, accelerating the four modernizations," Chiao-mu highlights the *objective nature* of economic laws based on the point of Marx. "Economic laws are like natural laws, and no natural law can be eliminated. What can change, in historically different circumstances, is only the way in which these laws are affirmed" (Chiao-mu, 1978). Based on the above, he criticizes the erroneously understood politics in command principle during Cultural Revolution, which has its most obvious failure in the Third Front and its economic consequences. In this same speech, he states:

> Due to our inappropriate understanding and dissemination of these instructions, and especially due to the pernicious influence of Lin Biao and the Gang of Four, there are still a considerable number of cadres directing economic tasks in the industry and agriculture, who still do not recognize in practice the objective nature of economic laws, refusing to take them into account. They take the will of society, the government and the authorities, as an economic law that can mold to political expediency; this is, as they understand it, the meaning of politics in command of the economy. These comrades forgot that "politics is the most concentrated expression of economics", and that on economic laws of objective existence, politics by itself cannot create other laws and impose them on the economy. In fact, as far as economic laws are concerned, the mission of the correct political leadership of the Party is precisely to make the maximum effort to ensure that our socialist economic task operates within the scope of these objective laws (as demonstrated in practice, this is a complex and arduous task). (Chiao-mu, 1978)

Given the exhaustion of the mass line as the axis for national construction that prompted the previous debate, reformists and intellectuals replaced the politics in command premise by a new logic that will end up imposed within the bureaucracy of the Party, hallmarking a new era of unparalleled economic growth and development in China: *the economy in command*. Having these favorable conditions, the reformist intellectuals operated organically with the reformist fraction of the Chinese bureaucracy that was in position to formulate a national project, articulating a set of historically excluded social classes. This implied a process of Passive Revolution, led by the rising reformist bureaucratic class and its organic intellectuals, which entailed the weaving of a new Hegemony in order to integrate the development aspirations of social classes until then excluded, reconfiguring the Chinese Historic Bloc.

This reconfiguration of the Historic Bloc implied a double process of rethinking the functions of the central bureaucracy and the expansion of the Bloc to incorporate the bourgeoisie of Greater China, separated from the mainland since the establishment of the People's Republic of China in 1949. On the one hand, the reformist bureaucracy headed by Deng Xiaoping pragmatically promotes its project of transition to a mercantile capitalist economy in close alliance with the local and regional bureaucracy, which, unlike the main hegemonic role-played by the central bureaucracy in planning, had played a marginal role during State economy. The strategic planning of development in China was the new commitment for central bureaucracy in accordance with the economic projection of a new reality. An important task for them is the capitalist management of State companies located at the top of the value chains. State companies generally have a military origin from periods like the Third Front, when significant financing channeled to develop science and technology for the defense of Chinese territory, creating telecommunications, automotive and solar energy companies.

Central bureaucracy manages financial capital—still centrally controlled by the Chinese State—based on the creation of new monetary and fiscal instruments, as well as the regulation of the internal market. Among their tasks are also price regulation, subsidies to certain productive sectors and the conditioning of foreign capital to access the Chinese domestic market, in terms of associating with national, State or private companies, thus promoting technology transfer processes and the consequent rise of national companies in the value chains of global productive networks. Meanwhile, regional bureaucracies promote development in regional economy, particularly through towns and villages companies, establishing small rural industries through which peasants became entrepreneurs in a short period. During nineties of the twentieth century, these rural companies represented more than 30% of the continental industrial product and began to fund local schools, welfare, health and transportation programs.

On the other hand, the process of expanding the Historic Bloc carried out the incorporation of the overseas bourgeoisie settled in the group of countries of the Asian Pacific basin. The coastal strip of southern China, between the Pearl and Yangtze rivers deltas, has a deep migrant tradition. Traders from the Pearl Delta region, which includes the provinces of Canton and Jiangxi, emigrated since the third century, fleeing the repression of the various imperial dynasties that dominated their territory and escaping natural disasters. These commercial refugees who speak various dialects (Wu, Hakka, Hokchiu, Hokkien, Teochiu and Cantonese), wove networks of commercial and business contacts (guanxi), shielded from Western penetration by their dialects and their sense of loyalty and belonging to their families and places of origin.

The return of this bourgeoisie to mainland China from 1979 to the first half of the nineties of the twentieth century meant the entry of billions of dollars to the Chinese economy, of which 80% came from Chinese capitals settled in the Asian basin. In 1995, the "gross national product" (GNP) of the 55 million transoceanic Chinese was around 450 billion dollars, 25% higher than the GNP of mainland China. Besides, a group of millionaires from Shanghai escaped from Chiang Kai-shek and Mao Tse-Tung in 1949 beginning a great exodus to Hong Kong. Those who fled represented China's business and financial elite, bankers and industrialists with generations of experience in the economy. Together with many descendants of the refugees from the Pearl and Yangtze rivers deltas, constitute transoceanic Greater China (Seagrave, 1995), and both of them found a place in the reconfiguration of the Chines Historic Bloc driven by pragmatism.

Reformers promoted the integration of the transoceanic bourgeoisie in the lower and medium chains of the global productive networks, establishing in China during the seventies of the previous century and becoming a major force in the economy since the mid-eighties. That was through the processes of relocation and global subcontracting of production that took place particularly in the Special Economic Zones with the establishment of American, European, Japanese and Asian companies enabling processes of learning and industrial promotion and integration of Chinese companies into global productive networks. During the early nineties, Sino-foreign joint ventures accounted for approximately 85% of total foreign direct investment (and 75% of total value) (Pearson, 1997).

Meanwhile, since the mid-eighties, the number of wholly foreign-owned companies increased. These enterprises do not involve any Chinese investment and foreign investors preferred them to keep a greater degree of control of operations and technology. However, they account for just under 15% of all foreign direct investment. There were approximately 70,000 joint ventures and wholly foreign companies registered in China by 1992 across a wide range of industries, encompassing the manufacturing of computer equipment, chemicals and pharmaceuticals, automobiles, consumer goods (mainly toys, bicycles, televisions and textiles), along with commercial companies and financial and real estate services as well. At the end of 1995, total foreign investment was around 400 billion dollars in more than 258 thousand companies (Pearson, 1997).

Finally, reformist bureaucracy built a new commitment with subaltern classes and groups, based on new opportunities and prospects for employment and economic development, which take shape with the increase in income wages. In addition, small local and village businesses as subordinate groups based on family relationships that do not imply workforce hiring represent the set of rural economic activities in their stage of mercantile economy in transit toward capitalism.

5.3 Chinese Competitive State Toward a New World Order

Based on the reconfigured Historic Bloc under reformist Hegemony, a new development pathway was plot in China with a new State economic–spatial development strategy. Between 1976 and 1986, a period of transition began from a centrally planned economy to a mercantile capitalist one, in which the State laid the foundations for a progressive ascent from the lower and middle links of the global production networks to the highest links of the value-added chains. The main economic reforms promoted by the restricted State, this is the Chinese Communist Party as the synthesis of political society, were carried out in the agricultural, industrial, banking and commercial spheres. This set of reforms, briefly described below, meant a process of Passive Revolution carried out mainly by means of coercion and with the aim of reducing China's vulnerability in the global market to concrete its passage toward its own modality of development under national premises.

The Fourth Plenary Session of the XI Central Committee of the CCP held in September 1979 outlined the agricultural reform adopting the domestic production responsibility system. This is a method of quantifying work allowing its remuneration based on its results, that is, a reorganization of agricultural production, similar to that existing before the establishment of the People's Republic of China, displacing the communal agricultural system. Thus, Revolutionary Committees dissolved in 1980 and Provincial People's Governments created, separating the responsibilities and political–administrative powers from those specifically linked to production. These changes resulted in a double organizational structure, on the one hand, the institutional organization of brigades and production teams through which the authorities implement agrarian policy and on the other hand, an agricultural sector around families and their new associative forms such as the cooperatives for the purchase of inputs and production sales, which gradually consolidated a mercantile system in the Chinese countryside as follows.

Having the family as the nucleus of central organization, groups of families formed teams, which together with others belonged to a production brigade. From this initial form of organization were derived at least three agricultural systems that appeared successively. First, the "production quotas agreed with groups" put into practice in 1979, where the production brigades established an agreement with groups of five to six families of the team provided with land, fertilizers, seeds, agricultural tools and farm machinery. The agreement established production levels whose degree of compliance determined bonuses or penalties in the remuneration within the team. Groups could dispose the surplus production totally or partially. This formula applied from 25% of the teams in 1979 to 11% of them in 1981.

A second form of organization began to work in 1980, known as "production quotas agreed with the families," where the agreement was established directly between the production brigade and the families, ignoring the level corresponding to the group and covering this formula to 78% of the teams in 1982. Third, "quotas of exploitation agreed with the families" or "integral exploitation quotas" began in 1981. This was a system similar to the lease, where the families no longer commit themselves to obtaining production quotas but to deliver to the team certain amounts as taxes to the State, planned quotas in the economic plan and mainly, as payment for the services provided by the team (machinery, social, educational, health services). However, the possession of the land is still collective and belongs to the commune or the village, and the farmer holds the right to use the land where is assigned to.

The period for which the right to exploit the parcels is granted has increased, from between three and five years, to fifteen years or more. In addition, the need to make an increasingly efficient use of land has led to the transfer of land between families, weakening collective property and rising specific agricultural productions such as livestock and horticulture (prohibited during Cultural Revolution as capitalist activities), the commercialization of generated surpluses and other activities such as handicrafts, basketry and shoemaking. Thus, specialized families have appeared that individually or jointly contribute to the opening of new productive and commercial forms in rural areas.

Later, the Third Plenary Session of the XII Central Committee of the CCP decided in October 1984 to outline a strategy to manage and strength the industrialization process following the next seven guidelines to State economic–spatial action. First, the State defines the strategy and the general objectives, appoints and dismisses the leaders and managers of the companies, granting autonomy in decisions related to production, supply, marketing, prices, investments and personnel, in order to operate as economic units that pursue profits. Second, coordinates the development plans of different regions, provinces and companies. Third, goes from controlling to regulating the economy, allowing the prices of a greater number of products determined by the forces of supply and demand instead of centralized control. Four, develops a macroeconomic control mechanism through taxes, interest rates and monetary policy under an improved financial and banking system.

Five, establishes various forms of "economic responsibility systems" between individual companies in order to promote efficiency, as well as establish differentiated wage rates to compensate for different types of work and levels of productivity. Six, launches large projects and key industries, promoting the development of collective and individual enterprises as complements to State enterprises. Finally, the State controls exchanges and defines relations with foreigners, expands international trade and investment to promote technological exchanges with foreign countries. Thus, State shaped a new industry organization in three sectors defined according to the degree of State intervention: directly administered sector, producer of strategic goods for the development and security of the country; indirectly controlled sector, of interest for economic development; and sector outside the State control, supplying the population's consumption. Table 5.3 shows the composition of each sector, its level of State intervention and its contribution to gross industrial product.

Table 5.3 Chinese industrial organization in the transition stage

Business sector	*Composition*	*State intervention*	*Contribution to gross industrial product (%)*
Directly managed	Large companies producing coal, wood, steel and basic chemicals	Direct, setting production and distribution targets to other sectors or between regions	25
Indirectly controlled	Medium-sized capital goods and chemical sector companies	Indirect, setting general guidelines for its development and intervening in its management by setting prices, credit conditions, taxation, labor regime, etc. Mixed economy instruments in general	50
Free of control	Small companies in the textile, footwear, clothing, etc., sectors	–	25

Source Own elaborated with information from Banco Exterior de España (1986)

This new configuration weakened the internal political organizations of the company and strengthened the power and autonomy of managers, in the perspective of a deepening of entrepreneurial capitalist management. Another step forward took place in 1987, with the introduction of the "contractual liability system" in all State-owned companies. In this system, each State company signs a contract with the level of government that has control over the company. Under the contract, the company agrees to pay the government a fixed annual tax, being able to withhold all remaining profits. Ten years later, the XV Congress of the Communist Party decided to restructure State enterprises into stock companies.

The same Third Plenary Session of the XII Central Committee of the CCP that carried out industrial reform outlined the price system reform. The main objective was to gradually deregulate the administrative determination of prices and allow their determination by market forces, through a succession of stages that eliminate the distortions maintained by planning. Due to the impossibility of releasing prices immediately, the solution was to introduce a two-tier system where a set of goods splitted in controlled and market prices. State regulated the increase in prices of raw materials and some intermediate goods, stabilized the prices of products widely used in production and consumption through subsidies and tax advantages, and eliminated subsidies for basic needs trying to keep the purchasing power of wages.

Thus, State-owned enterprises could still buy the assigned quantities of inputs and sell pre-established quantities of output at regulated prices. Additionally, each company could buy additional inputs and sell product, out of quota, at prices determined by the market. This system was into practice in a transitory period that mainly covered the second half of the eighties of the twentieth century. As time progressed, the administrative prices gradually changed until they coincided with the market prices. Toward the nineties, the two-tier price system began to disappear as most products in China sold at market prices.

Meanwhile, the reform of the financial system initiated in 1978 placed the People's Bank of China under the direct control of the Council of State with ministerial rank. People's Bank became central bank in 1983 assuming the tasks of monetary issuance and regulation, supervision of banks and financial entities, State treasury and administration of exchange activities. Specialized banks were established, including the Industrial and Commercial Bank of China, the Agricultural Bank of China, the People's Bank of China for Construction and the Investment Bank. These banks granted relative autonomy to offer credit during the first half of the eighties as well as the State industrial companies granted autonomy to make production decisions. Besides, State authorized installation of foreign banks until 1985.

Taking advantage of backwardness, State trade reform focused on two fundamental objectives: first, to achieve the modernization of industries from the deepening of commercial and economic relations, incorporating more developed technologies and new business management methods and second, to ease the integration of the bourgeoisie settled outside the continental territory, primarily in Hong Kong. On the one hand, foreign investment was attracted through tax, financial and labor incentives, as well as infrastructure and raw materials, requesting in counterpart, funds, technology and capital goods from the foreign investor for joint ventures enterprises.

On the other hand, State created the Special Economic Zones in 1980 selecting preferential locations for foreign investment, allowing their economic organization according to market economy. The SEZs represent authentic enclaves of the capitalist economy that permeated the rest of the economic system, strategically located in the areas of influence of important production and business poles such as Hong Kong and Taiwan. The first four SEZs promoted were Shenzhen and Shantou, near Hong Kong; Zhuai with Macao; and Xiamen off Taiwan. Provided with infrastructure, the Shenzhen Economic Zone attracted foreign investors who set up factories taking advantage of cheap and skilled labor, paying workers market-determined wage rates, different from the rates prevailing in other parts of China. Additionally, investors received special reductions in tax rates. In less than a decade, Shenzhen developed from a farmland area to a modern city. Due to economic differences, Chinese citizens could only enter Shenzhen with a special permit.

Having that experience, in 1985, State declared fourteen coastal cities (Dalian, Qinhuangdao, Tianjin, Yantai, Qingdao, Lianyungang, Nantong, Shanghai, Ningbo, Wenzhou, Fuzhou, Canton, Zhanjiang and Beihai) with industrial tradition as pilot centers to attract foreign investments, thus becoming export platforms to provide foreign exchange to the country and becoming regions that stimulate environment through diffusion of its effects, facilitating the introduction of reforms.

Based on the previous reforms, China integrated into global production networks during the eighties and nineties of the last century inserting itself into the low-tech and labor-intensive phases of production. Although this kind of productive insertion into the stages of lower technological demand had a reduced impact on China's technological development, it meant the beginning of a constant rise in global value chains. In order to achieve this goal, Chinese State deployed a set of economic instruments to promote electronic and telecommunication technologies industries since 2000 as the driving branches of the new phase of capitalist development

The set of financial support programs and subsidies carried out by the State to technology-oriented small, medium and large companies, as well as the constant strengthening of the education and scientific system, began to have a positive impact on the formation of joint ventures technology companies in mainland China. Among the available benefits considered in these support programs, Naughton (2007) describes the following:

- *Tax exemptions*: deductions for research and development expenses, exemptions for all income from the sale of new technologies and related consulting services and exemptions for the import of equipment used in research and development not available in China.
- *Subsidies*: support funds for small and medium-sized high-tech companies, an interest payment subsidy for specific projects of large companies, and coverage from the Import and Export Bank for high-tech exports.
- *Procurement preference*: National high-tech companies have preference in government purchases. In some cases, government procurement policies specifically support the development of the electronic industry.
- *Special fiscal and financial provisions for corporations*: accounting regulations in the calculation of capital adapted to allow inventions and intellectual property to account for as investments. High-tech firms can reserve 35% of the net value of increased assets for the purchase of financial options or other benefits for innovators and entrepreneurs. A small but active industrial venture capital sector is established with most of the funding coming directly or indirectly from government agencies, but also with a significant role for some foreign venture capital investors.

- *Positioning of national technology standards*: Chinese public policy designers promote and use local technology standards to generate competitive advantages for national companies.

Companies that initially relocated manufacturing processes in China were progressively more dependent on high-tech services, including research and development. Compared to the previous decades, manufacturing is a smaller fraction of the production process, and at the same time, the increase in the sophistication of the manufacturing process has increased the demand for design tasks and other capabilities. Because of this dual process, new opportunities have opened up in outsourcing knowledge-intensive services, such as software, engineering, as well as research and development. In this way, the encouragement of the Chinese State to the education and scientific system contributed, in a constant and consecutive way, to the insertion of the country in ever higher stages of the global value chains. China's integration no longer occurs only at the level of labor-intensive activities, but in tasks that also include engineering capabilities at medium and high levels, thus climbing in the inter-industrial and global division of labor.

Since 2011, the State established the promotion and development of key productive sectors of the electronic and telecommunications technologies as well as other cutting-edge technological sectors, grouped into seven emerging strategic industries: new information and communications technologies (development of broadband, Internet security infrastructure and software on the cloud; manufacture of high-end equipment (aerospace and telecommunications); biotechnology (drugs and advanced medical devices); new advanced materials (rare earths and semiconductors); vehicles powered by alternative energy (development of batteries and their components); alternative energies (renewable such as wind, solar and hydroelectric, as well as nuclear energy and biofuels); and energy saving and environmental protection (Ramo, 2011).

As a fundamental step to promote emerging strategic industries, Chinese State has strengthen telecommunications infrastructure. During the eighties of the twentieth century, the country invested only 0.2% of GDP in telecommunications, having at the end of that decade one telephone line for every 100 inhabitants. This changed in the nineties, when the State increased investment in this area close to 1.5% of GDP in 1993, keeping it constant in the following years. Thus, at the end of 2004, China had 312 million fixed lines and 335 million mobile lines, the largest telephone network in the world. While, in this year, the number of both fixed and mobile telephone lines per 100 inhabitants was practically the same as shown in Fig. 5.3, during subsequent years, the growth of mobile lines increased substantially, exceeding by 20% the number of the population in 2019. Due to the rise of mobile networks, the number of fixed lines tended to decrease. Despite the increase in access to mobile telephony, the percentage of the population with internet access was barely above half in 2017 (see Fig. 5.3).

Moreover, in order to reduce its dependence on foreign research and development, Chinese government and companies have invested heavily in recent years. In 2011, R&D spending was $139 billion or 1.8% of GDP. This budget was higher than the combined budget of France, Germany and the United Kingdom. Similarly, in 2011, China became the country with the highest number of domestic patent applications, surpassing Japan and the United States. As real growth in R&D spending has exceeded 18% since 2000, expenditure as a percentage of GDP has increased progressively, consecutively closing the gap with the United States (see Fig. 5.4).

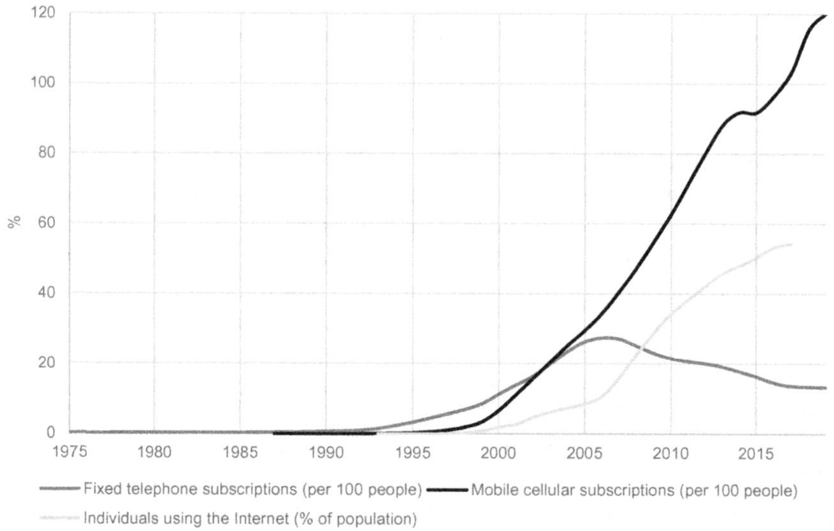

Fig. 5.3 Fixed and mobile subscriptions, and use of Internet in China (*Source* Own elaboration with World Bank data)

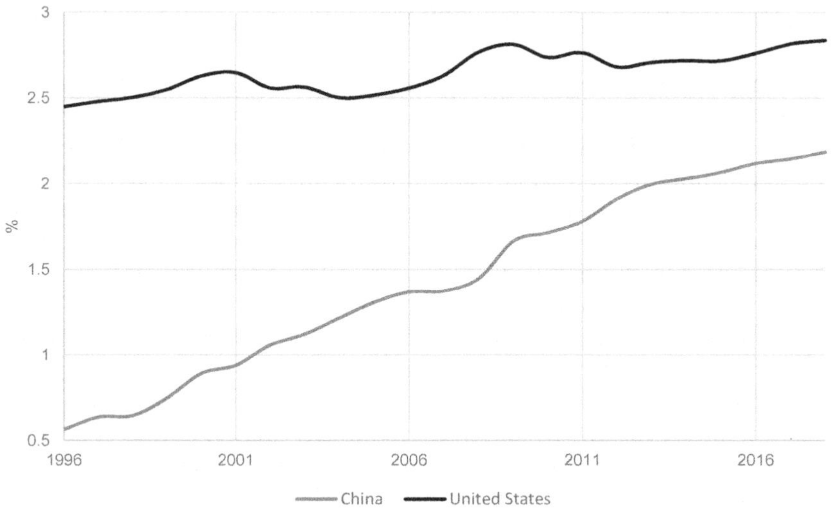

Fig. 5.4 Research and development expenditure as percentage of GDP in China and the United States (*Source* Own elaboration with World Bank data)

The transition in China from a statist economy to a mercantile capitalist one also meant a new State spatiality. The Maoist regime privileged the centrality of the national scale in restricted terms, as well as regional differentiation in integral terms. In the restricted State spatiality, the CCP was characterized by using the indivisible power of the State to control various areas of the population's socioeconomic–spatial relations, driving local and regional scales to interrelate based on statist planning logic with the centralized national scale. This planned operation of the economy rested on a hierarchical scalar system, composed of vertical links and coordinated by the large urban centers. At the top of this hierarchical system, large cities developed because of concentration of investment in infrastructure and agglomeration of economies, becoming nerve centers of the State planned economy, in order to maintain control and territorial integrity. At the base of the system were towns and villages, dedicated to the production of basic goods for consumption in large cities and war supplies.

This combined action led to the continuous expansion of large cities and the compression of towns and villages as is observed in the decreasing number of scales with less than 200 thousand inhabitants between 1949, when 102 villages housed little more than 25% of the population, and 1978, when 93 towns concentrated 14.1% of the population. In contrast, during this period, there was an increase in towns of medium and large size with more than 500 thousand inhabitants, where more than 60% of the population distributed at the end of the period (see Table 5.4).

In the integral sphere of spatiality, Maoist mass line development pathway determined State strategies regarding the spatial deployment of institutions. On the one hand, during the Third Front period, the military strategy drove the orientation of resources for development of scales far from the vulnerable coastal zones. On the other hand, ideology inhibited development of the southern and eastern regions, considering these traditional commercial regions as a residue of the capitalist system. This led to a differentiated spatial selectivity in the Chinese territory in order to promote development and industrialization in regions of the interior of the country, mainly in the north and northeast, and depress growth in China's southeast coast regions (see Fig. 5.5).

A first approach to this spatial selectivity is the regional construction capital investment in Chinese state companies, throughout the five-year planning periods as shown in Fig. 5.6. In the first four Five-Year Plans which cover from 1953 to 1975, a constant concentration of more than 30% of construction capital investment is shown in the north and northeast regions, except for the Third Five-Year Plan that coincides with the period of the Third Front, in which the southwest region received an increase in investment flow. In the same period, the southern and eastern regions of China did not add up to 20% for the same indicator, and in the

Table 5.4 Evolution of the space scalar system in China 1949–1978

Size of the city (Millions of inhabitants)	*1949*		*1978*	
	Number of cities	*Population (%)*	*Number of cities*	*Population (%)*
<0.2	102	25.5	93	14.1
0.2–0.5	18	19.8	60	23.4
0.5–1.0	7	18.7	27	25.0
>1.0	5	36.0	13	37.5
Total	132	100.0	193	100.0

Source Adapted from Lin (1999)

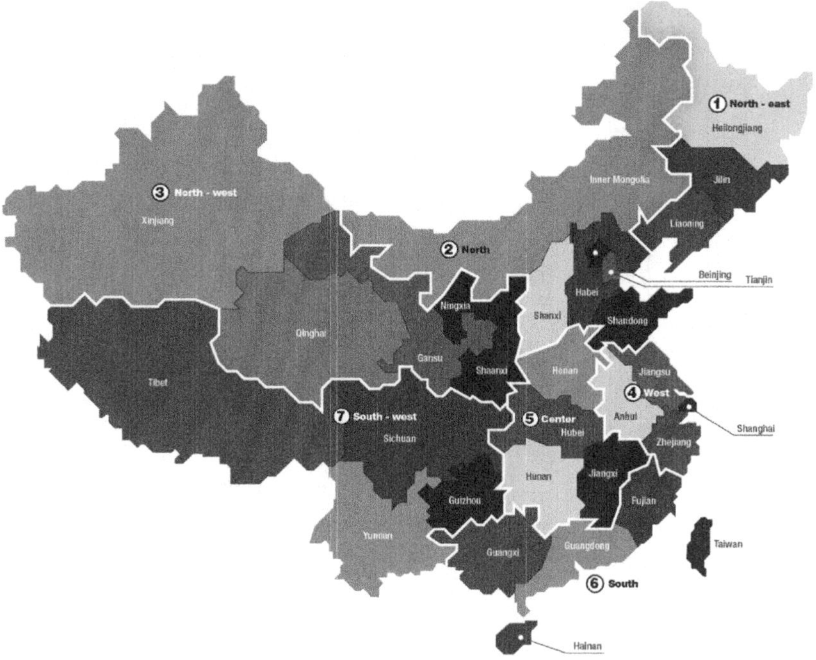

Fig. 5.5 Regions of the People's Republic of China (*Source* Lin (1999))

period of the third Five-Year Plan, there was a sharper decrease in the flow of construction capital for State-owned companies, caused by the Third Front military strategy.

This State spatiality to impact positively on the north and northeast regions, and negatively on the south and east regions, gave rise to an uneven geographical development. Thus, this unbalanced regional development was the result of the mass line development pathway of the State, which sought the accelerated advance of the north, inhibiting the development of the south.

China's transition to a mercantile capitalist economy ended the old north–south differentiated spatial State selectivity and opened a fast emergence of new economic regions in the south and east of China. In a new spatial selectivity, the State activated strong commercial ties between the first four Special Economic Zones located in Guangdong and Fujian

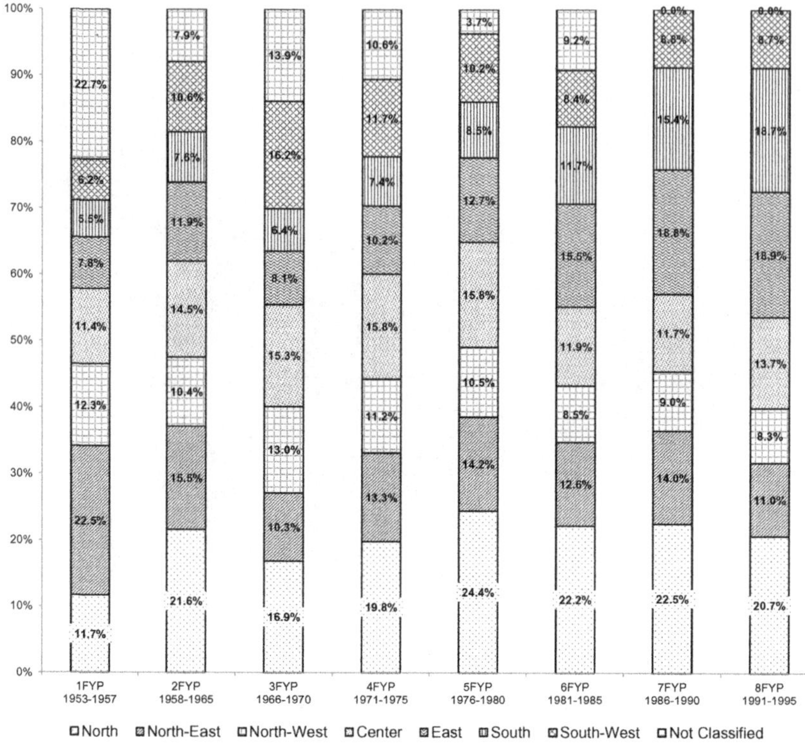

Fig. 5.6 Construction capital investment in Chinese State companies by Five-Year Plan and region 1953–1995 (*Source* Author's own creation based on Lin (1999))

(south) as well as fourteen port cities designated as trade zones (south-east), with the overseas Chinese bourgeoisie settled in the Asian Pacific basin, thus inducing an accelerated economic resurgence in the southeast region and a stagnation in the north of the country. The evolution of the gross domestic product of different study regions shows this spatial pattern of development in Table 5.5. There was a decrease in the north and northeast regional relative weight in the Chinese gross domestic product between 1978 and 1995. Meanwhile, in the same period, the eastern region and mainly the southern region (base of the first SEZs), show significant increases in their contribution to national GDP.

Table 5.5 Distribution of Chinese gross domestic product 1978–1995

Region	*1978 (%)*	*1995 (%)*
North	21.54	20.77
Northeast	14.03	10.33
East	21.94	22.87
Northwest	6.16	4.74
Center	15.82	15.30
South	9.91	16.55
Southwest	10.60	9.44

Source Adapted from Lin (1999)

Thus, the new State spatiality uses specific competitive advantages of regions with strong historic foreign trade links to project the regions and the State on a supranational and global scale.

Furthermore, the new mercantile growth promoted the towns and villages' enterprises, revitalizing small towns' economic functions observing unexpected expansion and growth. Faced with this emergency, a new scalar system has been created, in which the market demand for products and services has increased the number of cities considerably, turning them into centers of commerce, consumption and recreation. The previous scalar arrangement, rigidly hierarchical, vertically linked, and organized to be functional to the political needs of the CCP yielded to a new scalar system of cities, horizontally linked around commercial exchange.

The number of cities increased from 193 to 640 between 1978 and 1995. Within this group, the fastest growing were populations with less than 500 thousand inhabitants (see Table 5.6). Now, towns and villages are home to an important set of population, becoming the fastest growing scalar space in the new spatial configuration. Meanwhile, large cities of more than one million inhabitants changed their main role played in the mass line development pathway, for a new role in economic development, hierarchical horizontally, with towns and villages in proliferation.

Nowadays, Chinese State is the result of a reconfigured Historic Bloc founded on a new Hegemony based on a strong political and economic axis, politically, through the alliance of the reformist bureaucracy with the intellectuals and the local and regional bureaucracies, economically, from the new alliance with the overseas bourgeoisie and

Table 5.6 Evolution of the spatial scalar system in China 1978–1995

Size of the city (Millions of inhabitants)	*1978*		*1995*	
	Number of cities	*Population (%)*	*Number of cities*	*Population (%)*
<0.2	93	14.1	373	21.3
0.2–0.5	60	23.4	192	29.0
0.5–1.0	27	25.0	43	14.8
>1.0	13	37.5	32	34.9
Total	193	100.0	640	100.0

Source Adapted from Lin (1999)

the emerging national bourgeoisie. Hegemony included a refunctionalization of the central bureaucracy and a new commitment with a future development perspective for the subaltern classes. Thus, State deployed a new economic action toward the transition to a mercantile capitalist economy involving a national development strategy which was carried out under the State control of financial capital and a strong condition to the expansion of international productive capital in the Chinese domestic market. This conditioning is mainly oriented to the alliance with national Chinese companies and technology and knowledge transfer policies, promoting the rise of national firms. This has also meant a new State spatiality, moving from the centrality of the national scale to an important autonomy of the southeast region and the strengthening of its commercial relationship with extra-territorial scales, and the reorientation of the spatial system between large cities and towns and villages, moving relatively from a vertical to a horizontal hierarchy.

These specific characteristics of Chinese development pathway far from neoliberalism distinguish Chinese State as a Competitive State. A super-structural construction driven by pragmatism to achieve its development objective but based on national premises resulting from the strong hegemonic capacity within the Historic Bloc. The Competitive State is also adaptive, reconfiguring its institutional and spatial characteristics to position itself at the forefront of the new phase of development and, moreover, instrumentalist, taking advantage of social and scalar imbalances to maintain and maximize a global advantage in the development career. Based on this development pathway, the Chinese Competitive

State generated favorable endogenous conditions for its economic takeoff in the global stage.

China is currently carrying out a strategy of promoting outward its national development modality through deploying the Belt & Road Initiative, which connects the continents of Asia, Europe and Africa through six economic corridors (China–Mongolia–Russia Corridor; New Eurasian Land Bridge; China–Central Asia–West Asia Corridor; China–Indochina Peninsula Corridor; China–Pakistan Corridor; Bangladesh–China–India–Myanmar Corridor), thus replicating in the developing countries of East Asia, Africa and East Europe, the initial form of Chinese insertion in the inter-industrial and global divisions of labor. This means from the low and middle value-added links, for the production of a set of goods and services, aimed at satisfying the growing internal demand of the Chinese market, increasingly oriented to strengthen its position in global value-added chains, particularly in the high links of cognitive value.

In this way, the Chinese State supports the development of a set of key technologies with potential multiplier effects in the electronics and telecommunications industries, such as artificial intelligence (AI) to which it will allocate by 2030 just over forty times the German budget for this technology by 2025 (De Miguel & Pellicer, 2019). According to the Development Plan for the new generation of artificial intelligence, the construction of an open and collaborative innovation system based on AI includes the deployment of a high-precision global navigation and positioning network to accelerate the implementation of 5G technology, as well as the development of quantum computing processors. The central goal of the Chinese Communist Party is to gain global leadership in AI in order to consolidate its role as an economic power establishing a smart economy and society by 2030 (China State Council, 2017).

The growing economic and political influence of the Chinese Competitive State on the supranational scale implies the dispute of the hegemonic role with the United States in its own International System of State Hegemony, as well as the transit of the global economy epicenter from the Atlantic to the Pacific. This contrast between predominant development pathways expresses in the Sino–American trade war, as well as the European Commission statement qualifying China as a "systemic rival" in 2019 (De Miguel & Pellicer, 2019). However, the relative better economic performance of China after the financial-productive crisis of 2008 as well as the health crisis caused by the COVID-19 pandemic places its development modality in a better position than declining neoliberalism as a viable national solution to be followed by other countries, paving the way toward a new World Order.

References

Banco Exterior de España. (1986). *La Economía China de la Revolución a las Cuatro Modernizaciones*. Madrid: EXTECOM S.A.

Bettelheim, C., Rossanda, R., & Karol, K. (1978). *China después de Mao. Materiales, análisis, documentos sobre la lucha política en la transición socialista*. Barcelona: El Viejo Topo.

Chiao-mu, H. (1978, November). Observe Economic Laws, Speed Up the Four Modernizations. *Peking Review, 21*(45), 7.

China State Council. (2017). *Notice of the State Council on Issuance of the Development Plan for the New Generation of Artificial Intelligence* (000014349/2017-00142). Retrieved from http://www.gov.cn/zhengce/content/2017-07/20/content_5211996.htm.

De Miguel, B., & Pellicer, L. (2019, March 17). El nuevo miedo de Europa se llama China. *El País*, 2–3.

Fairbank, J., & Goldman, M. (2006). *China: A New History*. Cambridge: The Belknap Press.

Lin, G. (1999, December). State Policy and Spatial Restructuring in Post-Reform China, 1978–95. *International Journal of Urban and Regional Research, 23*(4), 670–696.

Naughton, B. (2007). *The Chinese Economy: Transitions and Growth*. Cambridge: The MIT Press.

Naughton, B. (1988, September). The Third Front Defense Industrialization in the Chinese Interior. *The China Quarterly, 115*, 351–386.

Nee, V., & Mozingo, D. (1989). *Estado y sociedad en la China contemporánea*. México: Fondo de Cultura Económica.

Pearson, M. (1997). *China's New Business Elite: The Political Consequences of Economic Reform*. Berkeley: University of California Press.

Ramo, G. (2011). *El XII Plan Quinquenal de la República Popular China*. Shanghái: Oficina Económica y Comercial de la Embajada de España en Shanghái.

Seagrave, S. (1995). *Lords of the Rim. The Invisible Empire of the Overseas Chinese*. New York: G.P. Putnam's Sons.

Tse-Tung, M. (1972). *Obras escogidas de Mao Tse-Tung Tomo III*. Pekín: Ediciones en Lenguas Extranjeras.

CHAPTER 6

Brazil and Argentina: Hegemonic Crisis, Neo-Developmental State and Wasted Decade

The last rise of conservative political forces associated with neoliberalism in Brazil and Argentina was not a casual event, but the product of a long crisis of Hegemony that both countries share within their Historic Blocs since the first third of the twentieth century, deepening their situation of economic backwardness. This hegemonic crisis essentially characterizes industrial bourgeoisies inability to lead a development project under national premises, as well as agro-exporting bourgeoisies ability to invalidate and neutralize the impulse of the State to undertake national industrialization.

The blockade of ruling classes explains the historical failure of the economic–spatial action of the State to overcome the condition of backwardness in both countries during imports substitution industrialization strategy as a development modality during Fordism–Keynesian, as well as the economic–structural limits of neo-developmentalism in the new phase of development or Knowledge Capitalism, thus resulting in a lost decade for development and the rise of neoliberalism in both countries at the end of the last century, and a wasted decade and the establishment of bizarre forms of neoliberalism during the present century.

This chapter has five sections that present a temporal analysis of the economic–scalar action of the State in Brazil and Argentina resulted from the set of social forces that established three development modalities

C. M. Sánchez Ramírez, *Knowledge Capitalism and State Theory*, Palgrave Insights into Apocalypse Economics,
https://doi.org/10.1007/978-3-030-71411-6_6

distributed in five stages of industrialization throughout three development phases. The first three sections correspond to imports substitution pathway that covered two phases of development: outward industrialization during British Empire World Order and national industrialization by Passive Revolutions and exports substitution industrialization strategy during Fordism–Keynesian.

While the last two sections refer to two development pathways during the present phase: neoliberalism and neo-developmentalism. On the one hand, the withdrawal of the industrial policy of the State during neoliberal boom resulted from the alliance between ruling classes and international finance capital and on the other hand the differentiated attempts to neutralize this alliance by emerging developmental States. This difference derived in a relative greater political autonomy of the State in Argentina compared to Brazil to lead the development process, as well as the return of *Kirchnerism* in the first country and the establishment of a hyper-reactionary neoliberalism in the second during 2019.

6.1 Outward Industrialization During British Empire World Order

Brazil and Argentina began an outward industrialization process integrating into the international division of labor from the export of raw materials to central economies such as England, France, Germany and the United States, in the center–periphery spatiality of the British Empire International System of States Hegemony.

The engine of early industrialization in Brazil and Argentina was the boom in coffee plantations and livestock and agricultural production and export, respectively. Both activities developed light industries linked to the textile, clothing, footwear and food sectors (Baer, 2008). Gradually forming manufacturing nuclei of relative importance that produced for the domestic market in the case of Brazil (Marini, 1975), and an incipient sector around processing and conservation industries, such as refrigeration facilities, flour mills, oil companies, breweries, alcoholic beverages, wool washing factories, leather preparation, tobacco and agricultural machinery in Argentina.

In both countries, the deployment of physical infrastructure aimed at meeting the needs of outward growth accelerated, mainly transportation[1] and energy (railways and power plants), financed by the agrarian bourgeoisie in association with foreign capital, particularly from Europe. In the case of Argentina, this encouraged the establishment of ancillary industries: railway material repair shops and construction materials industries and to a lesser extent, machine tool factories such as lathes and milling machines (Ikonicoff, 1980).

This incipient industrialization was driving in both countries by landlords and agro-exporter ruling classes. The Historic Bloc in Brazil formed mainly through the following social groups: agrarian bourgeoisie, rising entrepreneurs belonging to the agrarian bourgeoisie in search of diversifying their investments outside agriculture and playing a complementary role to the export sector. Imports traders or commercial bourgeois who knew local market characteristics and immigrants who integrated a new industrial working class. Immigrants were a key social group for the subsequent consolidation of the industrialization strategy by imports substitution due to their role as potential consumers of manufactured goods.

Meanwhile, in Argentina, the Historic Bloc formed by landlord and agro-export bourgeoisie as a hegemonic fraction and their organic intellectuals positioned in the upper links of the government bureaucracy, Parliament and the Courts of Justice. This group of intellectuals made up of a select group of men from the University of Buenos Aires who belonged to the landowner class related to livestock and agricultural activities forming bureaucratic elites mainly of lawyers at the service of the dominant fractions. The middle classes inserted in the lower links of the bureaucracy and were in charge of implementing the public policies designed by the elite. The dominant fractions of the Bloc opened a future perspective for these classes through the "bureaucratic career", controlling employment policies and directing part of public spending toward increasing a greater number of bureaucratic positions.

[1]The most important effect of the entry of capital into Argentina, mainly British (65% of the total around 1860), was the installation of a railway network of more than 34 thousand kilometers by 1914. Built to meet the needs of commerce, the rail network converged on the port of Buenos Aires, with a ratio between the length of the tracks and the surface of the pampas of 25 square kilometers for each kilometer of track, equaling the rail density of the United States and exceeding that of England and Belgium at that time (Ikonicoff, 1980).

In this stage in Argentina, the dominance of the hegemonic fraction is based mainly on coercion, so the army predominates as an instrument of the landowners to carry out their hegemonic project. This link of origin explains the historical relationship between landowners and the army in Argentina, as well as the active intervention of the latter in politics. The army became a transmission belt of domination from the hegemonic factions over the middle classes, as well as a vehicle for them to access better economic conditions and social prestige. Finally, the subordinate classes were made up of landless laborers, laborers and workers from an incipient and little concentrated industry (generally linked to farmers–tenants) who sought economic benefits by inserting themselves in the lower parts of the value chains of the outwards growth model.

Resulting from the set of practices of the dominant classes to maintain and justify their dominance toward the rest of the social fractions, during this stage, a liberal–oligarchic State formation took place in both countries. In Brazil, the "State of Compromise" (Marini, 1975) allowed the coexistence between the dominant fractions of the rising agrarian and industrial bourgeoisie, easing a cyclical development strategy for the mutual benefit of both groups. Thus, the exchange rate served as the central link in a series of events that began with its appreciation, caused by a combination of trade surpluses and capital imports from the agricultural export boom, thus making the imports of capital goods cheaper and promoting the expansion of the productive capacity of the industrial bourgeoisie. The subsequent devaluation of the exchange rate because the deficit in the balance of payments combined with the effects of an expansionary monetary policy worked as a barrier against the importation of finished goods, as well as a protection measure for the local manufacturing sector (Villela, 2011). This State formation lacked an active participation in the industrialization process as well as a national development strategy, allowing the integration of the Brazilian production system to the central economies based on the world market and not on its internal market (Baer, 2008).

In the case of Argentina, the actions of the State during this stage correspond to the interests of the landowners and the commercial bourgeoisie, linked to the financial groups of world capitalism. This meant a policy of promoting free trade, propping up purchasing power to sustain the volume of imports, limited industrial development and reluctance to reform the land tenure system. Thus, the promotion of the export sector was a priority to allow an increasing volume of imports and customs revenues. Foreign investors enjoyed preferential treatment from the Argentine government. Direct investments and loans channeled to the country in such a way that as Ikonicoff (1980) and Allub (1974) argue, between 1913 and 1914, half of the fixed capital in Argentina was in the hands of foreigners. They financed an important part of the railway infrastructure necessary for the export growth model and half of the country's debt corresponded to that contracted with external financial groups such as Baring, Rothschild and Morgans, among others, limiting the economic development of the Argentine nation[2].

During twenties in the twenty century, the industrial bourgeoisie gradually gained greater preponderance and independence from the agrarian bourgeoisie in Brazil. Some industries emerged outside the circle of influence of coffee cultivation such as cement, rubber products, agricultural machinery, iron and steel, paper, silk and other textiles, having an industrial production growth at an average of 5.4% between 1919 and 1929 (Villela 2011). The progressive advance of industrialization brought with it the emergence of numerous and complex social groups, particularly a growing middle class, as civil and military bureaucracies, directly affected by the exchange rate depreciation policy, in addition to the commercial bourgeoisie (importing merchants), and industrialists with interests opposed to coffee growers, who together exerted significant pressure on the State.

This pressure led to growing social unrest, limiting the exchange mechanism that made possible the profitability of the coffee sector and the viability of outward growth, thus configuring a serious problem of overproduction that since 1906 the State tried to combat through a

[2] In 1900, foreign investments in the country reached the amount of 2.5 billion dollars at the purchasing power of 1960, a figure that rose to 10.5 billion in 1913. The external debt was so big that a large part of the capital accumulated by the country through the exporting economy remitted, by way of amortization of interest and debts, to foreign usurers. This debt represented between 30 and 50% of the value of Argentine exports (Allub, 1974).

complicated strategy of valorization of coffee[3]. Finally, the difficult situation of the agricultural sector deepened with the world crisis of 1929: While coffee production presented increasing rates, exports of the product hardly absorbed two thirds of it. Despite the increase in real income in central countries, the demand for coffee remained stable[4].

Under this crisis scenario, the 1930 Brazilian revolution and the rise of Getúlio Vargas to power, backed by military–political movement known as tenentism and the growing urban middle class, linked to the gradual industrialization process, meant the re-composition of the specific weights within the Historic Bloc. Thus, revolution results from the struggle between the ruling classes and the rising social groups emerged from the modernization process of the country's economic structure, mainly through imports substitution industrialization, accompanied by a growing trend of masses participation in political life.

The transformations that took place in the economic structure expressed socially in the rise of an industrial bourgeoisie directly linked to the internal market, a new middle class and a new proletariat that together exert pressure on the historic dominant groups to obtain their own place in political society. The organization of the political–economic power of the oligarchic liberal State conditioned by the primary export economy began to take a turn from the reformulation of the operating conditions of the internal relations of production, thus as well as the relationship between the Brazilian economy and the international economy (Ianni, 1971; Marini, 1975).

Meanwhile in Argentina, the 1929 crisis and central countries protectionism meant the exhaustion of a development pathway as an agro-exporter peripheral economy. However, this did not led to revolution as in the case of Brazil, but to the deepening of conflict among social

[3] In order to reestablish the balance between supply and demand for coffee, Brazilian State implemented the "valorization" mechanism in 1906 to intervene in the market to buy surpluses. Foreign loans financed these purchases covered by a new tax on the quantity of exported coffee. In order to solve the problem of overproduction in the long term, the governments of the producing States had to limit the expansion of plantations (Furtado, 1974).

[4] In the United States, the main importer, where real per capita income increased by nearly 35% over the course of the twenties of the past century, coffee consumption remained at around 12 lb per capita although prices retail were stable. Prices paid by the American consumer in 1929 were no higher than in 1920 and slightly lower than in 1925 (Furtado, 1974).

classes within the Historic Bloc configured as follows. The landowner–agricultural bourgeoisie and particularly its commercial–financial fraction as a hegemonic class grouped in the Argentina Rural Society (SRA), favorable to the idea of a limited industrial growth functional to their interests. Breeders or ranchers displaced as a subordinate fraction of the agricultural bourgeoisie, grouped mainly in the Confederation of Rural Associations of Buenos Aires and La Pampa (CARBAP), against any industrial growth project considering it a risk to their own group interests. The tenants, small and medium agricultural producers nucleated in the Argentine Agrarian Federation (FAA), against the speculative nature of the dominant bourgeoisie and in favor of an agrarian reform (Murmis & Portantiero, 2004; Peralta, 2007).

The industrial bourgeoisie also divided. On the one hand, the "traditional" industrial bourgeoisie strongly linked to the productive activities of the agro-exporting landowning bourgeoisie. They were large companies nucleated in the Argentine Industrial Union (UIA), which took participation through financial capital, mainly foreign, as a mediator of investments in agriculture and industry, in a situation of subordination and acquiring a functional role to the interests of the hegemonic group. On the other hand, the emerging industrial bourgeoisie in growing conflict with the hegemonic group for the transfers of income from the agrarian sector required for their takeoff. It supported the expansion of the internal market, defended protectionism and called for the deepening of the industrialization process by imports substitution from the intervention of the State, but lacked a corporate or political organization with specific weight to allow them to channel their group progress aspirations (Murmis & Portantiero, 2004; Peralta, 2007).

As for the subaltern classes, mainly the workers, they were in clear confrontation with the hegemonic fraction of the bourgeoisie, the agro-exporting landowning bourgeoisie, which they associated with the super-exploitation of farm workers. Workers had an affinity with the emerging industrial bourgeoisie and its development and were against both the decrease in employment and the public sector, demanding a wage increase as well as social benefits provided by the State. Furthermore, the union organizations grouped around the General Labor Confederation (CGT) were in favor of the implementation of radical changes in the land tenure regime.

Under this social forces correlation forming a corporate Historic Bloc, due to the channeling of class interests through corporations, a second moment took place in the first stage of the industrialization process in Argentina between 1930 and 1943. This was a limited industrialization strategy, enough to replace imports of manufactured products but controlled in order not to alter the economic structure of the country, focused on agricultural exports. The rise to power of the State of the agrarian bourgeoisie dominant fraction through a political team drove government decisions from the beginning of the thirties until 1942.

In order to keep its predominant role, they promoted the signing of the Roca–Runciman pact between Argentina and Great Britain in 1933. The pact guaranteed the continuity of exports without restrictions of chilled beef from Argentina, as well as the freezing of customs duties for products imported from Great Britain. In reaction, the industrial groups in alliance with subordinate classes carried out a pressure campaign toward the government, which led to a set of protection measures for the sector by the State, summarized in a Plan of Economic Restructuring. The Plan included a control of foreign exchange for imports as a compensatory measure for the devaluation of the Argentine peso, which had favored the exporting agricultural bourgeoisie and made more expensive the acquisition of raw materials abroad by industrialists (Murmis & Portantiero, 2004).

6.2 National Industrialization by Passive Revolutions During Fordist–Keynesian Phase of Development

The second stage of imports substitution industrialization in Brazil and Argentina occurs within the broader framework of the Fordist–Keynesian phase of development, going through WWII and in the middle of the involved countries reconstruction in Europe and Asia, with a strong role of the State and under the forceful leadership of the United States, which emerges as the only great capitalist power in the world with an enormous economic, financial, political, and military scientific force. Rouquié (1989) refers to the second stage as "national industrialization or inward growth" that took place from 1930 to around 1960 with subperiods.

In the case of Brazil, the second stage of industrialization process took place between 1930 and 1964; meanwhile in Argentina, it starts until 1943 to 1965. Revolution accelerated the rearrangement of social forces within the Brazilian Historic Bloc between 1930 and 1936, being increasingly necessary to include the interests and progress objectives of a group of subaltern classes such as the emerging middle class and the proletariat, pointing to industrialization as a way to increase real income and consumption of the population. Meanwhile in Argentina, the industrialization process sped up because of the exhaustion of limited industrialization model (1930–1942) promoted by agrarian bourgeois and the progressive dissatisfaction of social groups of increasing importance in the national economy such as small- and medium-sized industrialists and workers. The stagnation of the real wage despite the increase in the labor force demand evidenced the secondary role that limited industrialization assigned to the increase in popular consumption (Peralta, 2007).

From 1937 to 1950 in Brazil and from 1943 to 1955 in Argentina were periods of Passive Revolutions backed by displaced industrial bourgeoisies and workers' demands. That is to say, the subaltern classes within the Historic Blocs boosted the project of national industrialization allowing the State to get a relative political autonomy from export–agrarian bourgeoisies, absorbing the social interest to promote the national industrialization project based on a new economic–spatial State role. This was a situation where the State replaced the class in the attempt of industrialization. They were not the hegemonic fractions that lead it, as it was an objective contrary to their class interests, nor industrial bourgeoisies, still incapable to direct it. Both Passive Revolution periods include the rise of the so-called populist regimes. It was the *Estado Nôvo* (1937 – 1945) in Brazil resulted from a coup headed by Getúlio Vargas, and Domingo Perón democratically elected in Argentina from 1946 to 1955. The latter promoted the corporate organization of small- and medium-sized companies through the General Economic Confederation (CGE), as well as the participation of union corporations in order to promote a national development project.

The central objective of the State during this period was to create the bases for the reproduction of industrial capitalist accumulation through an imports substitution strategy as a specific Latin America development pathway during Fordist–Keynesian phase of development. To achieve this objective, the State implemented a set of Keynesian policies in order to expand aggregate demand such as investment in infrastructure, expansion of credit, investment in production, as well as welfare policies oriented to the reproduction of the workforce such as redistribution of profits and regulation of the price of labor. Thus, the action of the State becomes constant in the economy, promoting industrialization through its direct participation in the development process of a modern industry linked to the Fordist driving industrial branches: metallurgy, mechanical and chemical industries.

In Brazil, the emergence of the expansion of the economic role of the State involved a spatial selectivity to promote industrialization processes mainly in the central and southern regions of the country, associated with the exploration and transformation of natural resources such as oil, coal, iron and steel and electricity. In the case of Argentina, the industrialization process deepened during the forties through the production of consumer goods (food, textiles and clothing), household appliances, simple machinery, metal products, as well as industrial activities related to construction, reducing the participation of foreign capital to a historical minimum after the nationalization of public services[5].

Post WWII imposed a limit to first Passive Revolution industrialization periods, due to a falling demand for traditional Brazilian and Argentinian exports by the United States against competition from Africa and the progressive resurgence of Europe. The decrease in the amount of foreign exchange that agriculture provided to the industry to import equipment and intermediate goods, as well as the diversion from industry to agriculture of a greater number of resources contributed by the State to finance the model, strained social force relations within the Historic Blocs between the agro-exporter and industrial ruling classes.

In Brazil, the social conflict solved through a second period of Passive Revolution. The impulse of subaltern classes mobilizations resulting from the spread to the lower classes of the conflict between dominant groups allowed the State to expand its economic interventionism in order to accelerate the promotion of industrialization. This period included

[5] The Argentinian government implemented a policy of nationalization of public services and repatriation of public debt. Telephones, electricity and gas distribution companies and railways nationalized using in part the credit balances the government had with Great Britain from wartime trade. Foreign capital, which in 1913 was equivalent to 50% of total fixed assets in the country, fell to 5% in 1955. Remittances abroad of profits and interest declined from 58% to 2% of the value of exports between 1910–1914 and 1955. At the same time, the State created enterprises such as the FAMA, ALFA and ZONDA air navigation fleets, which connected different parts of the interior of the country with Buenos Aires or were engaged in international trade, and incorporated new ships to the State merchant fleet. These airlines unified under the name of Aerolineas Argentinas in 1950 (Ferrer, 2010).

the second government of Getúlio Vargas (1951–1954) and lasts until 1964. The National Bank for Economic Development (BNDE) guided important public resources to the National Highway Plan, establishing Petrobras as a State oil monopoly, as well as Electrobras and Embratel as State electric and telephone companies. Moreover, the State also increased public spending in health, food, transport and energy industrial sectors through Salte Plan (Evans, 1995; Knox, 2001; Marini, 1975).

In contrast, in Argentina, the conflict between the ruling classes tended to deepen resulting in a military coup in 1955. Until 1965, the economic growth models promoted by the two main dominant groups coexisted in open struggle. On the one hand, the agro-exporter bourgeoisie trying to impose the return of the limited industrial development model applied between 1930 and 1943. On the other hand, the dominant fraction of industrial bourgeoisie progressively linked to foreign capital, trying to impose a development model based on the most capital-intensive branches, with strong subsidies, high tariff protection and incorporation of foreign technology and capital. Both ruling classes were interested in neutralize, invalidate and deactivate the economic interventionism that the State had implemented to accelerate the process of national industrialization, especially the Peronism financial policy of subsidized credit aimed at strengthening the medium and small fraction of the industrial bourgeoisie, as well as the income redistribution policies oriented to the lower classes.

In both countries, the large industrial groups did not carry out a hegemonic process toward the rest of the social classes around national industrialization, but their progressive link with foreign financial capital deepened the distance with the small and medium-sized national companies and served them as a point of support to confront the agro-exporting bourgeoisie. Furthermore, the social welfare of the subaltern classes was unsustainable because of rising prices inflation. The increase in the industrial reserve army caused by the transfer of the peasants to the cities contributed to the stagnation of wages but a rise in food products that increased the cost of basic goods. This increase in inflation generated an important rise in the protest movements of the working class, which pressed to stop the fall in the purchasing power of wages.

6.3 Exports Substitution Industrialization Strategy

This crisis of Hegemony within the Historic Bloc solved again through "progressive in terms of industrialization" or developmental military coups in both countries, opening the third stage in the industrialization process that Rouquié (1989) proposes as a period of exports substitution started in 1960 onwards in the Latin America economies. The exports substitution implied an increase in the leading industrial branches exports such as metal products and petrochemical and the automotive industries, through a Triple Alliance State strategy (Evans, 1984) that mainly took place in Brazil. This strategy involved the agreement among State-owned companies, the dominant industrial fraction or "internationalized bourgeoisie" (Cardoso & Faletto, 1977) and multinationals in a scheme of nationalist accumulation, and with the possibility of also include the national industrial bourgeoisie as a fourth partner, but eroding State corporatism as subaltern classes' distinctive redistribution component during the previous stage.

The State promoted the expansion of the industrial capacity of State-owned and private companies through the installation of technologies developed in advanced countries, making an effort to adapt to local conditions, meaning the implementation of Fordism as an organization and direction of labor modality in the production line, also incorporating specificities according to the local work areas. The State also promoted industrial projects to produce locally the basic inputs for production, reducing the strong dependence of both countries on importing them, as well as a progressive release in the payment of taxes on imported inputs necessary for production such as steel, aluminum and paper.

In the case of Brazil, in order to industrialize the northeast of the Brazilian territory, the State implemented a strategy of spatial selectivity during the sixties and seventies. The Triple Alliance strategy achieved greater synergies in the petrochemical industrial sector, where there was a strong State presence of public companies such as Petroquisa, a Petrobras subsidiary. Together with multinationals, mainly American, local groups contributed their industrial experience and local knowledge, their bureaucratic rules and incentives, in exchange for a share of the profits. In other sectors such as mining, the State also promoted joint ventures with multinational companies, although they were less successful experiences in their attempt to integrate the local bourgeoisie. In the pharmaceutical and textile sectors, where the State had a weak industrial presence, it only acted as a financial partner through the BNDE to support and protect local industry, without making efforts to specify backward or forward linkages, or generating competitive advantages within national industry (Evans, 1979)

This third and final stage of the imports substitution industrialization strategy (meaning exports substitution) took place in Argentina between 1966 and 1975; meanwhile, in Brazil, this stage began in 1964, and it lasts until 1990. The international context in which this stage occurred is one of structural–economic exhaustion of the Fordist–Keynesian phase of development that involved the questioning of the Welfare State and the irruption of the financial sphere which excess of liquidity yielded the crisis of the Latin American debt during the eighties or lost decade. Within the Historic Blocs, the rise in international prices of agricultural products during mid-seventies strengthened the dominant position of the agro-exporting landowner bourgeoisies.

Both in Brazil and Argentina, the State subsidies policy to boost the development of the leading industrial branches intensified the struggle for the appropriation of income between the agricultural and industrial dominant classes. The Hegemony crisis within the Historic Blocs continued unsolved, due to the inability of the large industrial bourgeoisies to assume a leading role and build an alliance with the agro-exporting bourgeoisies in terms of growth expectations that opened for both groups a coordinated insertion into the Fordist–Keynesian phase of development. Furthermore, the industrial groups that benefited at this stage were mainly the largest ones with strong ties to foreign capital, widening the gap between them and weak national industrial bourgeoisies left out of integration. Added to the struggle between ruling classes was the rise of worker mobilizations because the constant fall in real wages caused by the elimination of the redistributive component of the State's welfare policy in this last stage of imports substitution.

To the weak hegemonic capacity of dominant industrial bourgeoisies to lead an industrialization process linked to its inability to organize collectively, privileging individual negotiation in practice (Schneider, 1995) adds what Sidicaro (1982) considers as one of the most characteristic features of the landowner and agro-export bourgeoisies: the power to override. Thus, the Hegemony crisis between ruling classes has two components. On the one hand, the inability of dominant industrial bourgeoisies to organize collectively in order to lead a project of national industrialization, as well as orient the whole of the social action around this. On the other hand, the power of the agro-export landowner bourgeoisies to invalidate and neutralize the State impulse to the historical industrialization project contrary to its class interests.

Given the condition of Hegemony crisis within the Historic Bloc in Argentina, the conflict processed through a new military regime between 1976 and 1983, which meant a regressive solution in terms of industrialization. The crisis of Hegemony and the establishment of this new dictatorship meant the cancelation of the economic interventionism of the State in the process of industrialization by imports substitution and the return of the traditional economic program of the landowner and agro-exporting bourgeoisie. The dismantling of the State's industrial policy placed agricultural activities first and agro-industries later at the center of the economic dynamics from which the country inserted into the world economic structure, thus eroding the possibility of strengthening the competitiveness of companies that operated on the frontiers of knowledge, such as electronic firms, which at that time were as advanced as in Korea and Taiwan.

Meanwhile in Brazil, after a fast process of industrialization based on huge amounts of physical investment financed through strong external indebtedness during the period known as the Brazilian "miracle" (1967 – 1973), economic growth remained during seventies but at a slower rate, until it reached practically zero in the early eighties with the outbreak of the Latin American debt crisis. The persistence crisis of Hegemony unleashed a media campaign against the military regime for its policy of alliance between State companies and multinationals that relegated to the background the role of local industry. Under signs of inefficient nationalization, over-expansion of public companies and excessive bureaucratization of the State, the displaced bourgeoisie fought for democracy and the return to civil regimes and a new economic liberalism to stimulate the private sector (Evans, 1979).

Under unsolved Hegemony crisis within Historic Blocs, economic actions of Developmental States became insufficient to lead national industrialization processes failing in this objective in Brazil and Argentina. Thus, the State would face conditions of internal weakness and disadvantage during the rise of neoliberal Atlantic–hegemonic development pathway that would impose a set of public policies synthesized in the Washington consensus aimed at eroding the active role of the State in the economy during nineties of twentieth century.

6.4 Rise and Fall of Neoliberalism During Knowledge Capitalism

The weak hegemonic capacity of both ruling classes, agro-exporting and dominant industrial bourgeoisies, to carry out a set of agreements and alliances with subordinate groups around national development projects, is replaced with the international financial capital alliance in order to get a viable financial sustainability in the long term, keeping their dominant role within its Historic Blocs. This agreement was not held under national needs for promoting the technological–productive base of the new phase of development or Knowledge Capitalism that emerged during the eighties, but rather maintaining the basic structural–economic foundations of primary exporting economies. This alliance represented the political component of the neoliberal insertion of Brazil and Argentina in the new phase of capitalism from a national capital weakness position subordinated to global financial capital. Thus, financial capital became the eroding carrier of the economic–scalar role of the State in the economy and a driving force to replace the State by the market as the most efficient national resources distributor agent.

In the case of Brazil, bourgeoisie dominant groups integrated by agricultural raw materials exporters as well as industrial groups linked to natural resources processing industries took shape in firms such as Ipiranga (oil), Fósfertil (petrochemicals), Vicunha (steel), Gerdau (steel), Votorantim (metals and cement) and infrastructure industries such as the Odebrecht and Andrade Gutiérrez groups (Boito, 1998), as well as the banking business of large agro-mining exporting groups such as Bozano Simonsen. This group had 19% of its assets invested in mining activities through 16 companies, 20% in the agricultural branch with five companies, 26% in commercial activities through 15 companies, 15% in the industrial agricultural sector with seven companies and 20% in the financial sector through seven companies (Henze, 1986). Financial groups also owned huge large estates, between 200 and 300 thousand hectares, such as Safra, Bamerindus, Bradesco, Itaú, Boa Vista and Unibanco (Stédile, 2000). Meanwhile in Argentina, stood out food processing companies such as Bunge y Born, Cargill, Contintental, Louis Dreyfus, La Plata Cereal, Asociación de Cooperativas Argentinas and Nidera (Peralta, 2007).

The alliance between national dominant groups and global financial capital transferred the industrial capacities developed during the imports substitution industrialization process to its field of influence from the economic action of the restricted State functional to its class interests. The State implemented the economic component of the alliance through the establishment of the Real Plan in Brazil and the Convertibility Plan in Argentina. Both implied the establishment of favorable macroeconomic conditions, particularly a fixed exchange rate with the dollar underpinned by high interest rates, for the transfer of State-owned companies, as well as productive capital in hands of small- and medium-sized industrialists that emerged during imports substitution in both countries.

The transfer of public capital to the allied local and foreign economic groups through privatization processes intensified during the nineties. In Argentina, it began with the sale of the telephone company (Entel) and air navigation (Aerolíneas Argentinas), continuing with the electricity, gas and State steel companies (Somisa) in 1992, as well as the oil company YPF in 1993. Other national assets transferred to private capital for their management under the logic of the market were mainly in the infrastructure sector: oil, railways, ports, highways, water, drainage, television and radio channels. Between 1990 and 1999, revenues from the privatization of State-owned companies totaled \$20 billion. Thirty three percent of this figure corresponded to the investment of local economic groups associated with foreign capital in most cases, and 57.4% was foreign capital investment alone. Meanwhile in Brazil, a select group of 59 investors belonging to the dominant bourgeoisie associated with foreign companies or investment funds took control of a set of State-owned companies in the iron and steel, mining and fertilizer industries which revenues totaled \$33 billion between 1990 and 1997 (Boito,1998).

Dominant groups displaced and forced small- and medium-sized entrepreneurs emerged from the imports substitution industrialization process to sell and open their companies to foreign capital or to a partial or complete replace of their productive activities by importing or reselling products that they used to manufacture. In Argentina, the merge and acquisition of private companies reached an accumulated amount of \$55.5 billion between 1990 and 1999. At the end of the twentieth century, the presence of foreign capital increased around 40% in industrial activities such as agricultural production, hydrocarbons extraction, petroleum derivatives and the automotive complex (Peralta, 2007).

These processes of national deindustrialization brought with them a progressive concentration of the economies in primary export activities, as well as a deepening of the trade balance deficits. For example, in the first case, 49% of exports in Argentina during 1998 corresponded to the 100 transnational exporting companies. Of the total merchandise exported, 46.5% belonged to agro-food companies, 26.7% to the automotive sector, 17.5% to the oil and mining industry, and 9.3% to other manufacturing companies (Peralta, 2007). While, in the second case, exports went from \$35.7 billion in 1992 to \$53 billion in 1997 in Brazil, and imports tripled, from \$20.9 billion to \$62.5 billion in the same period (Sader, 2013).

After a first period of relative economic expansion during the first half of the nineties driven by the privatization of State-owned companies in both countries, its abrasive effects on national industry capabilities resulted in economic growth low rates in the second half of the decade and an increase in unemployment and poverty conditions of subaltern classes. This situation worsened at the dawn of the new century due to devaluations of the Brazilian real and the Argentine peso that were carried out in order to boost agro-mining exports. Devaluations led to cancel the Real Plan and the Convertibility Plan, as economic tools of the alliance between national ruling classes and international finance capital, without this meaning the end of the political agreement.

6.5 Neo-Developmental State and Wasted Decade

The rise of popular mobilization summarized in Argentina in the slogan *¡Qué se vayan todos!* (Fire everyone!), made it necessary to incorporate the social demands of the subaltern classes without this implying a new correlation of forces, much less the solution of the crisis of Hegemony within the Historic Blocs. The nineties decade rising unemployment significantly increased poverty among the subaltern classes as a consequence of dismantled industrial and salaried working classes in both countries. Thus, creating the new *piquetero* movement in Argentina and the strengthening in Brazil of working unions as the Workers Central Union (CUT) created in 1983, and peasant organizations as the Landless Movement (MST) started in 1979.

The rise of a social bloc made up of impoverished middle classes, neighborhood movements, cultural collectives and the peasantry, allowed the weaving of new relationships between civil society and political society achieving a differentiated break with neoliberalism in both countries. This was a reorientation of national pathways through the so-called neo-developmental States since 2003, meaning a new action of restricted State based on agricultural–mining and oil income that mainly carried out an important social policy around the fight against hunger and poverty (see Fig. 6.1), in order to strengthen the internal market and boost consumption. However, the impulse of a renewed industrial policy continued to be avoided, instead giving a new breath to the ruling classes who carried out a centralization in the most dynamic branches of the economy through its alliance with global finance capital, taking advantage of the strong economic dynamism of China during the first decade of this century.

In Argentina, the development pathway reorientation tried to neutralize with greater determination than Brazil the alliance of the ruling classes with international finance capital through the nationalization of State-owned companies and a macroeconomic policy far from the Washington Consensus and implemented under national premises, removing inflation control as an indispensable premise for economic growth. In order to support both dominant and subaltern groups, the State split its field of action into two economic–scalar spheres. On the one hand, the State kept a depreciated exchange rate to boost exports and stimulate economic growth, enabling agro-exporting bourgeoisie and large industrial groups to lead the increase in agricultural manufactures exports

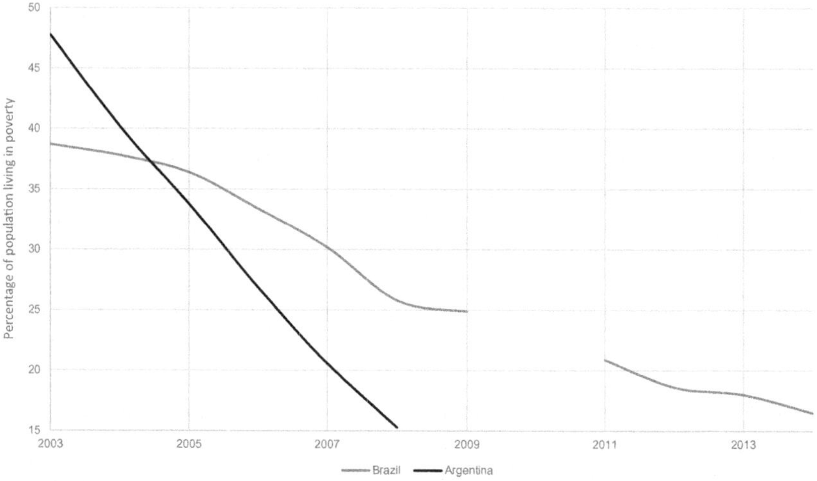

Fig. 6.1 Population living in poverty in Argentina and Brazil 2003–2014 (*Source* Economic Commission for Latin America and the Caribbean Statistics for Brazil and Repetto, F., & Potenza Dal Masetto, F. (2012) for Argentina)

at 12% average rate between 2002 and 2007 (Bastian & Soihet, 2012), although primary products and industrial commodities with low technological content prevailed. On the other hand, the strengthening of the State's social policy through the channeling of taxes on agricultural exports (the so-called *retenciones*) to expand the internal market opened the possibility for an incipient reindustrialization of the country based on the emergence of small and medium-sized enterprises mainly oriented to the national scale. They represent 90% of establishments and generate more than 70% of total employment, but unlike the large industrial groups, stay disconnected from international financial circuits having restricted access to bank credit and few links in global production chains (Fernández & Vigil, 2010).

The Argentine State broke most decisively with market efficiency ideology through renationalization of different State companies. Air transport Aerolíneas Argentinas and Austral previously in the hands of the Spanish group Marsans became State control in 2008. Distribution of drinking water and treatment of sewage liquids, Agua y Saneamientos Argentinos (AySA) acquired by the French group Suez, the Spanish company Aguas de Barcelona and the national group Banco Galicia, returned to State control by 90% in 2006. The remaining 10% was transferred to hands of workers, while the operational control is in charge of the Sanitary Workers National Federation. Radio–electric spectrum and satellite communication AR-SAT, controlled by the French company Thales Spectrum, is under State responsibility since 2004. Maritime transport Talleres Navales Dársena Norte (Tandanor) nationalized again in 2007, granting 10% of the shares to workers. Land transportation, Ferrocarril San Martín and the Roca and Belgrano Sur lines, is under State control since 2004 and 2007, respectively. In the hydrocarbon and oil industries, Yacimientos Petrolíferos Fiscales (YPF) was partially expropriated in 2012, and the new public enterprise Energía Argentina S.A. (Enarsa) was created in 2004. Regarding to postal mail service, Correo Oficial de la República Argentina acquired by the local Grupo Macri, it was taken over by the State in 2003.

Meanwhile, in the case of Brazil, there was no determined attempt by the State to break in the alliance of the ruling classes with finance capital as the foundation of the neoliberal agreement, maintaining a macroeconomic policy focused on controlling inflation as a condition for economic growth. There was also a strengthening of the ruling classes from an increase in the share of raw material exports as a percentage of the total, from 46% in 2001 to 55.4% in 2009. Unlike Argentina, Brazilian State development strategy oriented to national industry through small and medium enterprises was more limited as observed in an increase in the import coefficient in the industry, from 11.1% in 2004 to 19% in 2010. In the automotive industry, the import coefficient doubled in the same period, and in the textile industry, it practically tripled, while in the case of machinery and equipment, it increased by 65% (Bastian & Soihet, 2012). However, there was a promotion of State enterprises such as Petrobras and Embraer, as the latter supplies a large part of civil and military South America aircrafts market and is the third largest aeronautical company in the world behind Boeing and Airbus (Van Kleef, Ständer, Specht, & Hjorth, 2012). The most decisive action of the State was oriented to the subaltern classes through the *Fome Zero* (Zero Hunger) social assistance programs, reducing extreme poverty from 12% in 2003 to 4.8% in 2008, incorporating 20 million Brazilians to the middle class as part of the expansion of the domestic market (Van Kleef et al., 2012).

The absence of structural change in both countries was mainly due to the irresolution of the crisis of Hegemony within the Historic Blocs. The different degrees of rupture of the State with the international financial capital conditions, as the basis of the neoliberal alliance with the local dominant groups, allowed Argentina to obtain a greater margin of maneuver than Brazil to promote an endogenous process of development, thus resulting at a higher average rate of economic growth in the former than in the latter during the neo-developmental stage [see Figs. 6.2 and 6.3].

However, insufficient economic–spatial action of the State to overcome backwardness during neo-developmental period (2003 – 2015) which in Argentina corresponded to Néstor and Cristina Kirchner presidency as well as Lula da Silva and Dilma Rousseff in Brazil configures a ***wasted decade*** for both countries to overcome economic backwardness in the present phase of development, thus yielding the way to bizarre forms of neoliberalism as a declining pathway that briefly took place in Argentina before the return of Kirchnerism and established in Brazil with hyper-reactionary dyes in 2019.

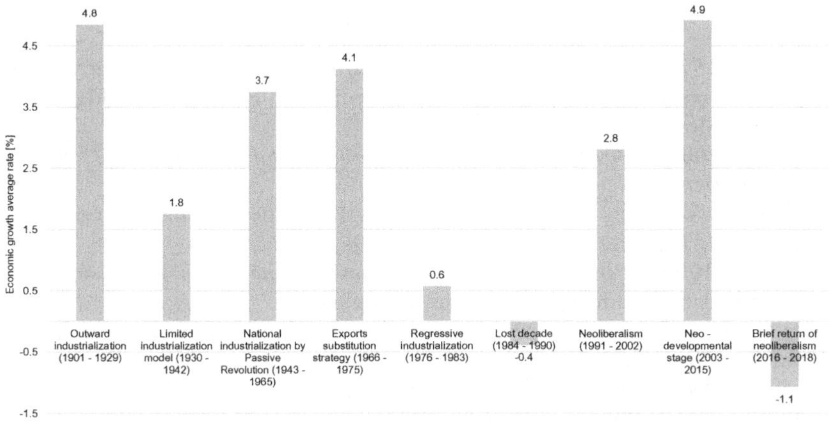

Fig. 6.2 Argentina economic growth average rate by development pathway stages 1901–2018 (*Source* Maddison Project Database (2020))

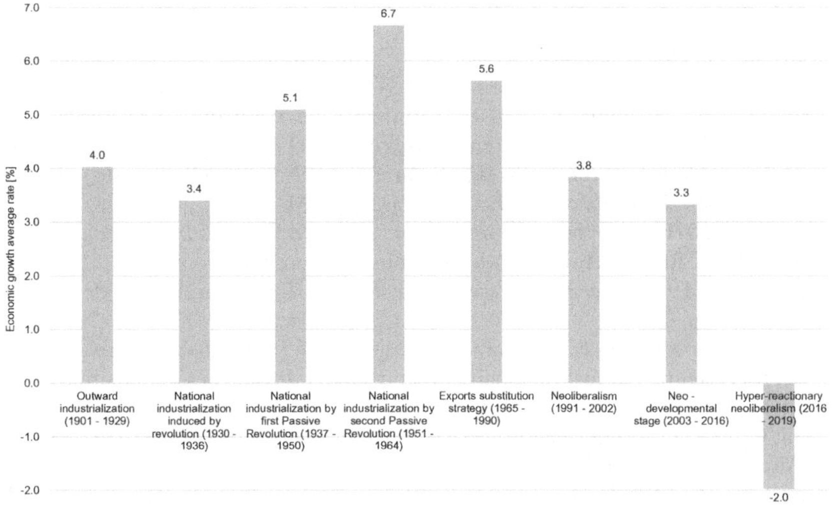

Fig. 6.3 Brazil economic growth average rate by development pathway stages 1901–2019 (*Source* Maddison Project Database (2020))

References

Allub, L. (1974). *Estado y sociedad civil: patrón de emergencia y desarrollo del Estado argentino, 1810–1936*. México: Centro de Estudios Sociológicos, El Colegio de México.

Baer, W. (2008). *The Brazilian economy: Growth and development*. Colorado: Lynne Rienner.

Bastian, E., & Soihet, E. (2012). Argentina y Brasil: desafíos macroeconómicos. *Problemas Del Desarrollo, 171*(43), 83–109.

Boito, A. (1998). *Política neoliberal e sindicalismo no Brasil* (Tesis doctoral). Universidade Estadual de Campinas, Campinas.

Cardoso, F., & Faletto, E. (1977). *Dependencia y desarrollo en América Latina*. Buenos Aires: Siglo XXI Editores.

Evans, P. (1995). *Embedded autonomy: States and industrial transformation*. Princeton, NJ: Princeton University Press.

Evans, P. (1984). El calzado, la OPIC y la indudable convicción: las empresas trasnacionales y las relaciones Estados Unidos – Brasil. En R. Fagen (Sel), *Estado y clases sociales en las relaciones Estados Unidos – Latinoamérica* (pp. 326–361). México: Centro de Investigación y Docencia Económicas, Fondo de Cultura Económica.

Evans, P. (1979). *Dependent development: The alliance of multinational, state, and local capital in Brazil*. Princeton, NJ: Princeton University Press.

Fernández, V., & Vigil, J. (2010). Estrategias de desarrollo y reconstrucción estatal: obstáculos y desafíos en la Argentina del bicentenario. En Alejandro Dabat. (Coord.), *Estado y desarrollo* (pp. 99–158). Ciudad de México: Instituto de Investigaciones Económicas, UNAM.

Ferrer, A. (2010). *La economía argentina: desde sus orígenes hasta principios del siglo XXI*. Buenos Aires: Fondo de Cultura Económica.

Furtado, C. (1974). *Formación económica del Brasil*. México: Fondo de Cultura Económica.

Henze, R. (productor) & Guimaraes, E. (director) (1986). *Bozano, Simonsen, 25 anos* (Documental institucional). Roland Henze Producoes Cinematográficas. http://youtu.be/ezoiVwIp2uU.

Ianni, O. (1971). *Estado y planificación económica en Brasil (1930–1970)*. Buenos Aires: Amorrortu Editores.

Ikonicoff, M. (1980). La industrialización y el modelo de desarrollo de la Argentina. *El Trimestre Económico., 47*(185), 159–192.

Knox, B. (2001). *Reassessing the impact of institutions on economic reform in Brazil*. A thesis presented to the graduate school of the University of Florida in partial fulfillment of the requirements for the degree of Master of Arts, University of Florida.

Marini, R. (1975). *Subdesarrollo y revolución*. México: Siglo XXI.

Maddison Project Database. (2020). Bolt, Jutta and Jan Luiten van Zanden (2020). *Maddison style estimates of the evolution of the world economy: A new 2020 update.*

Murmis, M., & Portantiero, J. (2004). *Estudios sobre los orígenes del peronismo.* Buenos Aires: Siglo XXI Editores Argentina.

Peralta, M. (2007). *La economía política argentina: poder y clases sociales (1930–2006).* Buenos Aires: Fondo de Cultura Económica.

Repetto, F., & Potenza Dal Masetto, F. (2012). Sistemas de protección social en América Latina y el Caribe. Argentina, *CEPAL-Sistemas de Protección Social en América Latina y el Caribe*, colección Documentos de proyectos.

Rouquié, A. (1989). *América Latina: introducción al extremo occidente.* México: Siglo XXI.

Sader, E. (2013). La herencia neoliberal de Cardoso. *Brasil. Avances y contrastes.* Buenos Aires: Le Monde Diplomatique.

Schneider, B. (1995). La burguesía desarticulada de Brasil. *Revista Mexicana de Sociología, 57*(4), 135–153.

Sidicaro, R. (1982). Poder y crisis de la gran burguesía agraria argentina. En A. Rouquié (Comp), *Argentina, hoy* (pp. 51–104). México: Siglo XXI.

Stédile, J. (2000). Latifundio: el pecado agrario brasileño. *Chiapas, 9*, 113–138.

Van Kleef, P., Ständer, P., Specht, S., & Hjorth, S. (2012). *Global Brazil and the political economy of the Brazilian model.* Roskilde: Roskilde University.

Villela, A. (2011). A bird's eye view of Brazilian industrialization. In W. Baer & D. Fleischer (Ed), *The economies of Argentina and Brazil: A comparative perspective* (pp. 38–65). Cheltenham: Edward Elgar.

CHAPTER 7

Post-pandemic COVID-19 World Order: Decline of Neoliberalism and Strike Back of the State? A Reading from Gramsci

The emergence of a new phase of development or Knowledge Capitalism during the eighties of the twentieth century involved the radical technological revolution carried out by the invention of the microprocessor and the development of software, and its articulation with Toyotism as a new form of organizational and labor management. This gave way to a new industrial revolution and the establishment of the electronic and telecommunications technologies as the driving industrial branches of this new phase, replacing the automotive, metal–mechanical and petrochemical complex of Fordism–Keynesian.

The impetus for this new technological–productive base came from the boom of financialization, particularly from venture capitals, which enabled a group of Schumpeterian entrepreneurs to conceive and design a series of merchandise with increasing cognitive value added. This process gave rise to an acceleration in the innovation rates and changed the economic dynamism from demand to supply, setting up a counter-trend to the falling trend in the rate of industrial profit in the crisis of the Fordist–Keynesian phase of development. Thus, it opened a new stage of boom and economic growth during the twilight of the twentieth century.

From these economic–structural elements, the rise of a new Historic Bloc in the United States took place. As dominant classes arose the Wall Street venture capitals groups in alliance with Silicon Valley entrepreneurs

C. M. Sánchez Ramírez, *Knowledge Capitalism and State Theory*, Palgrave Insights into Apocalypse Economics,
https://doi.org/10.1007/978-3-030-71411-6_7

and Hollywood creative industries, who managed to bring together a group of social movements made up of feminists, anti-racists, environmentalists and lesbian–gays, as well as social groups of Latinos, young people and African–Americans.

As subordinate fractions are the rest of the social groups linked to the old productive technological base of Fordism–Keynesian: industries related to manufacturing, extractive, military, small companies and their associated financial capital as well as nationalist, racist and homophobic movements of thought expressed in social groups of evangelical Christians, southern white population, rural and small town populations, and white working classes.

The establishment of this Historic Bloc let the Hegemony of dominant groups over the subalterns from canceling the redistributive role of the State in favor to the market via financialization. The core of a new common sense projected over the set of social classes that gave them a new perspective of future was the substitution of the State for the market, as the most efficient agent of resource distribution in different social spheres. That hegemonic process led to the preponderance of the political actions of the full State over the restricted State to constitute neoliberalism as an Atlantic–hegemonic development pathway.

Meanwhile, China undertook a different development modality in Knowledge Capitalism in the early eighties. Starting from a strong economic action of restricted State, it managed to insert itself first in the lower and middle links of the value-added chain, through the reproduction of goods belonging to the electronic and telecommunications technologies industrial branches, climbing progressively to the high cognitive value-added links. The specificity of China's development pathway, in which coercion prevails over consensus within the ruling class of the restricted State, has allowed it to become a global superpower, contesting the leadership of the United States on its own International System of States Hegemony, and in the process of building its own.

The global financial–productive crisis of 2008 or "market failure" deepened the questioning of subaltern groups about the viability of neoliberalism as a predominant development pathway on a global scale, causing fissures in the Historic Blocs and a crisis of Hegemony around the preponderance of the market and its economic–financial agents. Despite this questioning, the response to this market crisis has continued from its very foundations, via the injection by the main world Central Banks of trillions of dollars in the world market, based on the ineffective strategy of quantitative easing to revitalize the sluggish global economy.

The COVID-19 outbreak, as the first global pandemic, has highlighted different strategies of the States to contain the spread of the virus within national scales, as well as its institutional capacity to decrease the number of deaths among its population due to the novel coronavirus. This implies the contrast on a global scale between predominant development pathways—on the one hand, declining neoliberalism and its fragmentation into bizarre development modalities led by the United States, where ruling classes push for a fast and lethal spread of SARS–CoV–2 among its populations, in order to keep going the functioning of the market, on the other hand, State-led development pathways which find their most complete experience in China, where a slow spread of the virus tends to prevail, thus reducing the number of fatal losses among its population.

The deepening of the post-pandemic socioeconomic crisis arises questions around a new World Order to be born from the clash of States development pathways. Will it increase the erosion and fragmentation of neoliberalism, deepening the disintegration of eminently neoliberal economic scales such as the European Union? Will the Belt and Road Initiative and post-pandemic support plans to different Western Hemisphere countries accelerate the transition process of the world economy epicenter, from the Atlantic to the Pacific? Gramsci´s powerful theoretical lens and actual pandemic empirical evidence together with post-financial crisis health data let outline answers for these questions as follows.

7.1 Market Versus State: Depicting the Link Between Financial Productive Crisis (2008) and Pandemic Emergency (2020) in Distinctive Development Pathways

Using a time lapse between the financial–productive crisis of 2008 and COVID-19 global sanitary crisis, the main goal of this section is to gauge the return of the State or the advance of the market in the three main development modalities established in the previous chapters: neoliberalism, Nordic and developmental. In its space dimension, the analysis considers fifteen leading and following countries of the distinguished development pathways in three regions as shown in Table 7.1, thus taking advantage of Gramsci´s theoretical framework, as well as health spending

Table 7.1 State–market financial–pandemic crises case studies by development pathway and region

Region	*Development pathway*		
	Neoliberal	*Developmental*	*Nordic*
Americas	Mexico United States	Argentina[a] Brazil[b]	
Europe	France Germany Italy Spain United Kingdom		Finland Norway Sweden
Asia	Japan	China South Korea	

[a,b]The analysis considers the neo-developmental experiences of South America countries that took place in the first decade of the twenty-first century, in addition to recent returns to neoliberalism
Source Own elaboration

data and spread and lethality of SARS–CoV–2 during its first global strike until April 2020, and a vector chart builds to map the advance or retreat of the State vis-à-vis the market in the selected study cases between the market failure and the pandemic.

Two variables show the connection link between the global productive financial crisis of 2008 and the State's ability to manage the current health crisis caused by COVID-19 pandemic. The first is the full State, measured by the expansion or reduction of the State's health expenditure, as well as its capability to constrain market action, especially those of private health insurances. A World Health Organization (WHO) index that indirectly expresses the direction of the first component is the out-of-pocket health expenditure as a percentage of total health expenditure, which estimates the direct health expenditure made by households in each country, as a proportion of total health expenditures. The second is the restricted State, seen as its capability to minimize SARS–CoV–2 lethality.

The subtraction of the first index between the last available data (2017) and 2008 represents a proxy of the direction of State action in the field of public health after the financial–productive crisis. A positive subtraction indicates a retraction of full State after 2008 crisis, meaning a decrease of public and private resources aimed at public health, increasing the population health direct spending, leaving them in a situation of social vulnerability. While a negative subtraction indicates the expansion of full State after the crisis, meaning an increase of social, public and private resources, aimed at the health of the population, reducing the direct expenditure that population makes in health care, and the probability of falling in a situation of poverty and social vulnerability (see Table 7.2).

The second index is the proportion between the number of deaths and confirmed cases of COVID-19 as a proxy for the case fatality rate, showing restricted State capability to manage pandemic crisis. The contrast between both indices results in a State–market–financial–pandemic–crises vector (see Fig. 7.1). In general, the countries that obtain a positive difference in the first index between 2017 and 2008 meaning

Table 7.2 Case studies indices for health expenditure and COVID-19 pandemic

Country	*Health expenditure 2008 and 2017*			*COVID-19 pandemic 2020*		
	Out-of-pocket expenditure as percentage of current health expenditure[a] *[%]*		*Subtraction (2017–2008) [%]*	*Number of deaths*[b]	*Number of cumulative confirmed cases*[b]	*Proxy of case fatality rate [%]*
	2008	*2017*				
Argentina	25.6	15	−10.6	215	4,304	5.0
Brazil	30.9	27.5	−3.4	5,466	78,162	7.0
China	47.4	36.1	−11.3	4,643	84,385	5.5
Finland	19.5	20.2	0.7	211	4,995	4.2
France	10	9.4	−0.6	24,342	128,121	19.0
Germany	14.1	12.7	−1.4	6,288	159,119	4.0
Italy	21.3	23.5	2.2	27,967	205,463	13.6
Japan	15.2	12.8	−2.4	432	14,281	3.0
Mexico	48.6	41.3	−7.3	1,732	17,799	9.7
Norway	15.7	14.2	−1.5	204	7,710	2.6
Korea	37.4	33.7	−3.7	248	10,774	2.3
Spain	21	23.6	2.6	24,543	213,435	11.5
Sweden	16.9	15	−1.9	2,586	21,092	12.3
UK	9.4	16	6.6	26,771	171,257	15.6
United States of America	13.1	11	−2.1	55,337	1,035,353	5.3

[a]This index estimates how much are households in each country, spending on health directly out of pocket. It estimates the share of out of pocket payment of total current health expenditures *Source* https://apps.who.int/gho/data/view.main.GHEDOOPSCHESHA2011v?lang=en
[b]*Source* https://covid19.who.int/. As of April 30 2020

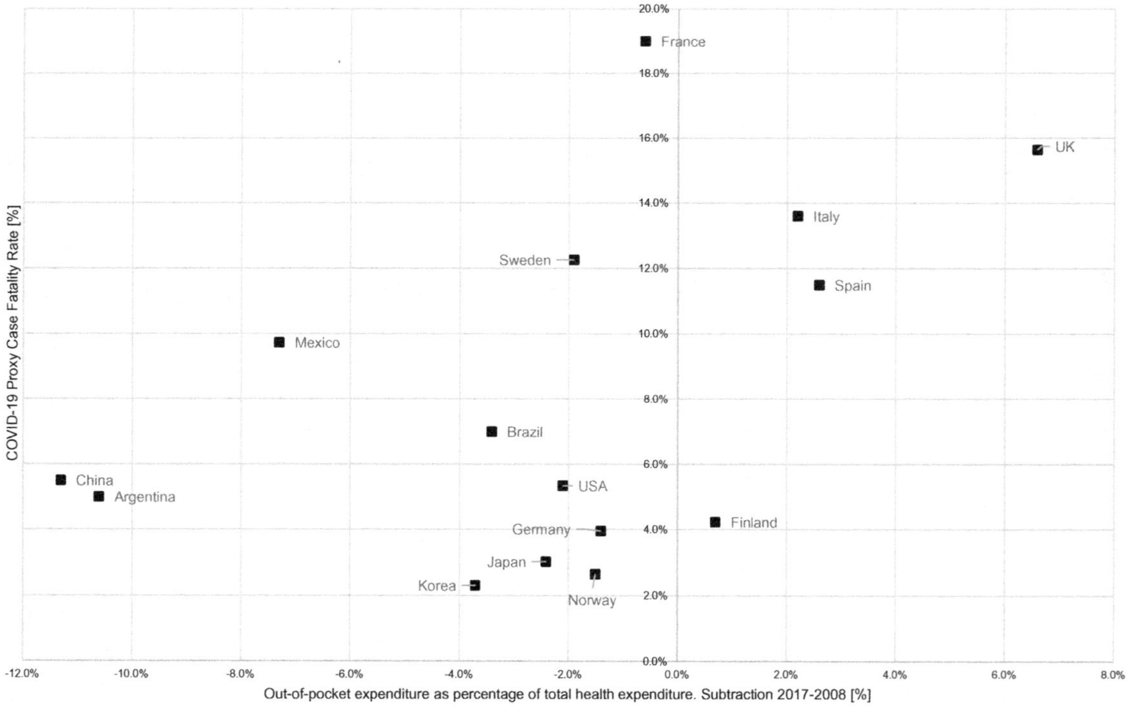

Fig. 7.1 State–market–financial–pandemic–crises vector (*Source* https://apps.who.int/gho/data/view.main.GHEDOOPSCHESHA2011v?lang=en, https://covid19.who.int/. As of April 30 2020)

the full State withdraw in the field of public health after the financial crisis present a higher second index (case fatality rates for the new coronavirus) of more than ten percentage points. Such are the cases of the United Kingdom, Italy and Spain. To a lesser extent is the case of Finland, which presents a lower case fatality rate (4.2%). While, in general, those countries for which the difference in the first index is negative meaning the full State expansion in the social resources allocated to public health have a lower second index (less than ten percentage points). Such are the cases of Germany and Norway in Europe; Japan, Korea and China, in Asia; and the United States, Brazil, Mexico and Argentina in the Americas (see Table 7.2).

The cases that are outside the second mentioned generality are that of France and Sweden, while the case of France observes a marginal reduction in the proportion between direct spending on health and total spending on health between 2017 and 2008, and—among the studied group of countries—it is the one with the lowest proportion of this first index (9.4% in 2017); it has the highest case fatality rate (19%) among all. Similarly, Sweden presents a decrease between the first index studied for 2017 and 2008, meaning a higher expansion of full State in public health, and very close to the case of Norway, its "Nordic Twin." However, it has the fourth highest case fatality rate among the group of countries considered (12.3%).

The mapping of the previous vector allows outlining initial reflections on the distinctive features of the struggle between the State and the market, as a dynamic process that primarily during the first novel coronavirus hit tended to flare up in the different modalities of development pathways. This dispute manifests firstly in the financial crisis of 2008 and now tends to have a greater importance and scope during the current pandemic unfolding. A guide to carry out this discussion is the location that studied countries have in the vector chart (see Fig. 7.1), combined with the SARS–CoV–2 speed propagation rates shown in Table 7.3, resulting in groups and subgroups as follows.

The first set of countries located in the right quadrant of the chart (see Fig. 7.1) are the cases of the United Kingdom, Italy, Spain, and Finland. The first three clearly affected by case fatality rates higher than 10% and high virus propagation (increases of 18.8% per day in average). In these cases, there was a significant withdrawal of the full State in the field of public health after the 2008 financial crisis (more than two percent points in each country). In this first group, the market logic tended to

Table 7.3 Case studies SARS–CoV–2 Speed Propagation Rates

Country	*[% per day in average as of April 30, 2020]*
United States	16.8
Germany	13.2
France	13.4
Italy	22.4
Spain	19.9
United Kingdom	14.2
Western Europe [Sample]	16.6
Finland	16.2
Norway	14.8
Sweden	17.6
Nordic Countries [Sample]	16.2
China	9.0
Japan	9.8
Korea	10.5
Asian Countries [Sample]	9.8
Argentina	18.1
Brazil	21.2
Mexico	17.8
Latin American Countries [Sample]	19.0

Source https://covid19.who.int/

prevail over the State in managing the health crisis, that is, a fast and fulminant spread of SARS–CoV–2 that would ease a rapid recovery of the economy. Thus, the State practically abandoned the implementation of any measure to contain the virus in its first stage of propagation, with the United Kingdom[1] being the most radical case in this regard, when trying to apply a (failed) "herd immunity strategy." Meanwhile, the cases of Italy and Spain belatedly began the confinement of their populations, after the WHO declared the novel coronavirus as a global

[1] The UK has only 4000 intensive care unit beds capable of treating severe cases, only 5000 ventilators, and it suffers a shortage of nurses after 10 years of government cuts to the health service. Moreover, the UK also no longer manufactures the type of ventilators needed to effectively treat severe coronavirus cases as other EU countries scramble to boost their own capacity. Smaller ventilators used to treat less severe respiratory conditions are made by the Brears factory in Stratford-upon-Avon, bought by China's Fosun Pharma in 2017 (Clarke, 2020, March 16).

risk (February 28, 2020). Italy did so eleven days after the WHO statement with thousands of accumulated confirmed cases (10,149). Spain started after fifteen days having 5 thousand, 753 accumulated confirmed cases. The United Kingdom joined the emergency confinement 25 days after said declaration, when it reached 11 thousand 658 accumulated confirmed cases.

The case of Finland becomes a relevant one because it shows an incipient Nordic development pathway "loss of momentum" or "neoliberalization process" as explained in Chapter 4. It presents a high speed of virus propagation (16.2% per day in average), close to the three previous countries' average. Moreover, Finland faint withdraw of the full State shows in a (marginal) increase of the proportions of direct expenditure of the population on health as a percentage of total expenditure on health between 2017 and 2008, having the higher index (20.2%) among the Nordic countries analyzed [see Table 7.2]. The Nordic country began relatively early strict measures of the confinement of its population comparing its number of confirmed cases with those of Italy, Spain and the United Kingdom (seventeen days after WHO statement with only 272 accumulated confirmed cases), marking a prevalence of the logic of the State over the market in the administration of the public health crisis. However, it has a relatively high case fatality rate (4.2%) bigger than Norway (2.6), showing certain weakness of the restricted State to manage the health crisis.

The second set of countries located in the left quadrant of the chart (see Fig. 7.1) are the study cases of Norway, Germany, Japan, Korea, China, the United States, Brazil, Mexico and Argentina, most of them affected by case fatality rates of less than ten percent, except in the cases of France and Sweden, which have a higher rate. In this set of countries, unlike the first, there is an expansion of the full State in the sphere of public health after the 2008 financial crisis, although with different scopes.

Among this second group are the "Nordic Twins," Norway and Sweden, which share geographical, cultural, economic and political similarities. The expansion of the full State in the field of public health from 2008 to 2017 is around two percent in both countries. However, in Norway—as the case of Finland in the first group—population mobility has been more severely restricted, while, in Sweden, the market logic of free movement tended to prevailed even up to April 2020. Further, Sweden has the second lowest rate of intensive care units (5.8) for every 100,000 inhabitants in all of Europe, only above Portugal (4.2), and below Norway (8), Finland (6.1) and the European average (11.5) (Rhodes et al., 2012). Moreover, the restricted State capacities deployment to manage the health crisis in Norway resulted in a lower speed of the virus propagation (14.8% per day in average) than in Sweden (17.6%) and Finland (16.2%). In relation to the case fatality rate, there is also a better performance from Norway than its "Nordic Twin" Sweden, while, in Norway, this index is 2.6%; in Sweden, it is almost five times higher (12.3%).

As part of this second group are the United States and Germany, both countries are promoters of neoliberalism as an Atlantic development pathway and architects of supranational scales of economic integration under the logic of free market, as the former North America Free Trade Agreement (NAFTA) and the European Union (EU) as well. Like the previous subgroup of Nordic countries, there is an expansion of the full State in the field of public health after the 2008 financial crisis of close to two percent in both countries. Both of them have low case fatality rates, Germany (4.0%) below the United States (5.3%).

Germany opted for early confinement in relation to the first set of countries analyzed, starting the suspension of non-essential activities (March 13) fourteen days after the WHO global risk statement, with 2260 accumulated confirmed cases, less than the half of those in Spain and no deaths. Accordingly, it has the lowest virus propagation speed among the all European countries studied (13.2% per day in average). Screening test application was extensive; besides, Germany has one of the largest health expenditures in relation to GDP in the European continent (8.9%), only behind Denmark (9.8%), and the highest index of intensive care units for every 100,000 inhabitants in all of Europe (29.2) (Rhodes et al., 2012).

In the case of the United States, despite the Law on Patient Protection and Health Care or "Obama care" played an important role in the expansion of the full State in public health, the United States became the epicenter of the pandemic, as well as the core of the contradictions on the health crisis management—on the one hand, the old automobile, metal–mechanic and petrochemical complex bastion (the so-called rust belt) and the global financial sector in the northeast of the country, striving for a solution that prioritizes continuity in the market operation, based on a fast and lethal spread of the virus and on the other hand, the southwestern region of the country and the state of California in particular, which houses Silicon Valley as a paradigmatic scale of the "glocal" or global center of innovation. This last region implemented a more restrictive set of measures regarding the confinement of its population, resulting in a case fatality rate of 4.1%, while the same index for the state of New York is 7.7% (USA Facts, 2020, May 1).

Asian countries, Japan, South Korea and China are also in this second set of countries, which expanded full State in the field of public health after the financial crisis of 2008 and until 2017. Japan presents an expansion of 2.4%, South Korea 3.7% and China 11.3%, and the three countries have the lowest SARS–CoV–2 speed propagation rate (9.8% per day in average) among all the studied countries. Japan has a low case fatality rate (3.0%). However, the dominant groups in the electronic, computer and telecommunications sectors strongly questioned the partial and gradual confinement measures that restricted State took to manage the health crisis. Industrial conglomerates like Sony, Toyota, Panasonic, Sharp and SoftBank (Lewis, 2020, April 21) demanded a solution to prioritize continuity in the operation of the market. The social conflict within the State in Japan reflects itself in the national emergency declaration made until April 16 and accompanied by a previously announced economic rescue package that reaches 20% of national GDP (Pesek, 2020, April 20).

In this subgroup of Asian countries, there are those where the State has played a relevant role in the process of national industrialization in Knowledge Capitalism, such as South Korea and China as studied in Chapter 5 in the second case. Both countries have low speed propagation rates (Korea, 10.5%; China, 9.0%) and low case fatality rates (Korea, 2.3%; China, 5.5%) and implemented different health containment measures in order to maintain market viability, without resulting in a fast and lethal spread of the new coronavirus. While South Korea did not enforced strict confinement, the State collected data by using cameras, smartphones and bank transactions to map the social relationships of suspected cases (Beaubien, 2020, March 26). On the other hand, China implemented strict confinement measures and activated a community management network from the division of cities into grids, zones, blocks and communities. These networks have social promoters who depend on the local authority and were responsible for monitoring social organization and stopping its activities, as well as providing aid to the elderly and the population with disabilities (SCMP, 2020, March 26).

Finally, as part of the second set of analyzed nations are the Latin American countries: Brazil, Mexico and Argentina, showing an expansion of the full State in the sphere of public health between 2008 and 2017 of 3.4%, 7.3% and 10.6%, respectively. In the study cases of Brazil and Argentina, it is significant that the expansion of the full State in the field of health increased during the neo-developmental periods, which emerged in the first decade of this century resulted from a strong social questioning of neoliberalism as explained in Chapter 6. The two South America countries have case fatality rates below ten percent (Brazil, 7.0%; Argentina 5.0%), but high virus speed propagation rates (Brazil, 21.2%; Argentina, 18.1%; per day in average). The first low indices probably link to the State-led strengthening of the public health sphere after the 2008 financial crisis, similar to the case of the United States. The recent return of Kirchnerism to the presidency in Argentina meant an administration of the pandemic crisis putting the interest of public health before the interests of the market. By contrast, in Brazil, the opposite phenomenon arose derived from the exhaustion of the neo-developmental experience and the rerouting of a neoliberal development pathway with hyper-reactionary overtones. The latter placed Brazil on the way to become the new epicenter of the pandemic.

In the case of Mexico, there was an increase in the participation of the State in relation to public health after the 2008 financial crisis (7.3%). However, the proportion of the direct expenses of the population in health as a percentage of total expenditures in this item continued to be very high (41.3% in 2017), meaning the highest proportion among all the countries analyzed here. Although the case fatality rate in Mexico is below ten percent (but a high virus propagation rate of 17.8% per day in average), it is rapidly approaching to exceed this threshold. The weakness of the State public health system and the flexible containment measures show a certain preeminence of the dominant economic groups that are committed to a solution via the market, mainly the mining, construction and automotive industries that were the first economic activities declared as priority by the government since June 2020 to break the confinement. This neoliberal contradiction shows itself with more emphasis in the northern region of the country. This scale hosts the Latin America's most dynamic export manufacturing industry of medical devices from transnational companies, which have been adverse to stop their activities or to maintain them by increasing security measures for their workers (Sánchez, 2020, April 30).

7.2 Decline of Neoliberalism or Strike Back of the State?

Since the financial–productive crisis of 2008, both subordinate dominant and lower fractions on a global scale questioned neoliberalism. For them in general, the prospect of a future projected through the market for all social classes had been broken, causing a crisis of the hegemonic capability within the Historic Blocs. This gave way to a situation of blurring and fragmentation of the basic principles around the preeminence of the market over the State as the most efficient distributor of available resources, the hegemonic core of the neoliberal pathway.

The analysis carried out in Sect. 7.1 shows the withdrawal or expansion of the full State in public health after the financial crisis and the ability of the restricted State to manage the pandemic emergency. Thus, the questioning of neoliberalism by dominant and subordinate social classes after 2008 led to an incipient return of the State, particularly in the three most important developed economies that undertook the neoliberal development pathway since the eighties decade of the twentieth century: United States, Japan and Germany. In the United States, as the main promoter of neoliberalism, the return of the State initially had an impulse from below after the 2008 financial crisis, contributed by a series of social discontent expressions that had their climax in the Occupy Wall Street movement. Furthermore, this tenuous return institutionalized precisely in the field of public health through the enactment of the Patient Protection and Affordable Care Act or "Obama care."

Subordinate dominant fractions of capital drove from above a second impulse. They belong to the automotive, metal–mechanic and petrochemical complex, as well as ultra-conservative social groups, for whom the free market has meant a position of subordination within the Historic Bloc. This neoliberal fragmentation with hyper-reactionary overtones, which is synthesized with the defeat of Bernie Sanders and the rise of Donald Trump to the presidency of the United States in 2017, fueled a process of economic disintegration of eminently neoliberal scales in order to get a better position in the economic field.

That economic disintegration process promoted by the Trump administration refers first to the withdrawal of the United States from the Trans-Pacific Partnership (TPP), as the main instrument engineered by the Obama administration to contain by consensus the growing influence of China in the Asia–Pacific region (Sánchez, 2016). Second to the renegotiation of the North American Free Trade Agreement (NAFTA), now, the United States–Mexico–Canada Agreement (USMCA) as a tool aimed at the reindustrialization of the “rust belt” in the northeast region of the United States. The urgency of a new economic boom in this dwindling industrial scale explains in part the resistance to sanitary confinement by the associated dominant and subaltern social groups, which, as discussed in Sect. 7.2, has resulted in a high COVID-19 case fatality rate compared to other regions within the United States and third, to the trade war with China, which meant a shift toward the field of coercion to try to contain the global influence of the Asian giant.

Meanwhile, in Western Europe, a second trail of countries that followed the neoliberal modality maintained or deepened it in its classic way after the 2008 crisis. The withdrawal of the full State in the public health field, as well as in the restricted State low performance in managing the health crisis, shows it. The most radical case is that of the United Kingdom, followed by the cases of Italy, France and Spain. In relation to the Nordic pathway, although there is a continuity in their development modalities led by Innovative States, the pandemic makes evident the disputes between dominant groups within the Historic Blocs, particularly those that demand for the need to increase the role of the market in the social sphere. An example of this process of “neoliberalization” of the Scandinavian countries manifests particularly in the different administration of the health crisis in the “Nordic twins”: Norway and Sweden, as well as the study case of Finland.

The Asian pathways considered as developmental have a deepening role of the State both in its broad and restricted sense, as the study cases of South Korea and China has shown in its well performance in managing the pandemic emergency. Unlike the supranational scales that suffer an economic disintegration process commanded by neoliberalism (TPP, NAFTA and EU), there is a boom of economic integration scales driven by alternative development pathways in Asia. China alone signed bilateral investment treaties with more than fifty countries to promote two-way investments, the Regional Comprehensive Economic Partnership (RCEP) in 2020, and expects to sign the China-EU Comprehensive Investment agreement soon. Further, China is able to project its development pathway on a global scale through the Belt and Road Initiative, which connects the continents of Asia, Europe and Africa through six economic corridors (China–Mongolia–Russia Corridor; New Eurasian

Land Bridge; China–Central Asia–West Asia Corridor; China–Indochina Peninsula Corridor; China–Pakistan Corridor; Bangladesh–China–India–Myanmar Corridor) (ACCA, 2017).

It is remarkable that China does not built the Belt and Road Initiative (B&R) as an exclusive multilateral cooperation agreement but as an open cooperation platform. B&R overlaps with another regional economic cooperation initiatives proposed by countries in the Asia–Pacific region, such as India (Multi-Sectoral Technical and Economic Cooperation Program or Bay of Bengal Initiative), Russia (Eurasian Economic Union), among others. Moreover, the withdrawal of the United States from the international scene in the sanitary crisis allowed China to strengthen its trade relations and global influence by sending material and human resources to nearly 200 countries (according with the Ministry of Commerce of China). In addition, China's National Health Commission has proposed deepen regional coordination in response to the epidemic, rearticulating scales of international cooperation, such as China–ASEAN, Shanghai Cooperation Organization, China–ARAB League and China–Central and Eastern European Countries, based on shared knowledge of issues related to the epidemiological outbreak.

In the case of the South America countries, Brazil and Argentina, the return of the restricted State in the social sphere during the neo-developmental period (2003–2015) is notorious in the relatively low COVID-19 case fatality rates. However, the insufficiencies in the economic and structural aspects during that period gave rise to the so-called wasted decade, which preceded the return of neoliberalism in both countries, although in Brazil with hyper-reactionary traces similar to the United States. The recent return of Kirchnerism in Argentina is an example of the continuous dispute between the dominant fractions of the Historic Bloc, particularly of the agricultural exporter groups and the social bloc made up of the middle classes, neighborhood movements, cultural collectives and the peasantry. Similarly, but in the northern part of the Americas, the recent rise of the electoral left in Mexico was accompanied by a critical discourse against neoliberalism, although with little evidence so far about profound changes in the correlation of forces inside the Historic Bloc. The ruling classes pressed to conclude with a non-restrictive national confinement that lasted a couple of months, managing to break it in June and obtaining the government declaration to give way to the continuity of mining, construction and automobile economic activities, all of them linked to the most important dominant groups in the country, thus resulting in a high virus propagation rate and a case fatality rate close to ten percent.

The financial–productive crisis and economic stagnation, as well as the pandemic emergency, both global phenomena, have imposed a need in the capitalist system to reorient neoliberalism as its preponderant Atlantic–hegemonic pathway. In this way, within the Historic Bloc of the United States, there is currently a struggle between fractions of dominant and subordinate classes for the need to incorporate a renewed State action that allows the following: first, to unlock the conflict between financial capital and productive capital, in order to redirect the extraordinary torrent of financial resources to the productive sphere. This would allow the impulse of emerging technological revolutions with radical capabilities such as artificial intelligence and quantum computing. That way, productive capital would drive a new stage of economic growth on a global scale, promoting the set of current industrial driving branches such as the electronic and telecommunications technologies, and revitalizing the industrial branches belonging to the industrial pattern of the Fordist–Keynesian development phase, that is to say, the automotive, metal–mechanical and petrochemical complex; second, to deploy an updated welfare State, which, based on a cognitive and inclusive orientation, facilitates the active incorporation of subordinate groups, based on the recognition of social conflict and the coverage of flexible forms of work, mainly oriented toward its cognitive valorization; and three, to have a determined participation to slow down the effects of climate change, with the aim of ensuring the viability in the medium and long terms of the capitalist mode of production itself. In addition, to include critical sectors of young people or *millennials*, who via their most visible representative at the United States Congress, Alexandria Ocasio–Cortez (AOC) demand the need to implement an environmental policy or Green New Deal.

That process would imply a Passive Revolution, which would allow neoliberalism to subsist as a development pathway, starting from the incorporation of elements of its antithesis. Therefore, neoliberalism could assume features of greater predominance of the consensus or full State, derived from the integration of State elements that are present in the experience of the Nordic development pathway, which would lead to a "keynesian – neoliberalism." Otherwise, it could assume features of greater predominance of coercion or restricted State, derived from the growing influence and supranational projection of the Chinese Competitive State, leading to bizarre or hyper-reactionary neoliberalism. Either scenarios will depend on the correlation of forces within each Historic Blocs of the three neoliberal capitalist powers, but the recent election of Joe Biden as president of the United States sets an important precedent to rearticulate neoliberalism via consensus.

Meanwhile, the China pathway, as the predominant route in the Asian basin, shows in general terms a more effective administration of the health crisis compared to classic neoliberal capitalist economies. This allows it to consolidate the particularities of its specific form of development led by its Competitive State and project them on the supranational scale from the following efforts: first, the attempt to move the epicenter of the global economy from the Atlantic to the Pacific through the deployment of the Belt and Road Initiative[2], which involves replicating in the developing countries of East Asia, Africa and East Europe, the initial form of Chinese insertion in the inter-industrial and global division of labor. It means from the low and middle value-added links, for the production of a set of goods and services, aimed at satisfying the growing internal demand of the Chinese market, increasingly oriented to strengthen its position in global value-added chains, particularly in the high links of cognitive value and second, the construction of a financial institutional framework, sterilized from the international speculative markets, that allows it to direct a set of financial flows toward the development of productive projects at national and international level, through the Asian Infrastructure Investment Bank, BRICS New Development Bank, Shanghai Cooperation Organization Development Bank, and the China–ASEAN Interbank Association.

The Chinese well performance in times of crisis provides the country with a better position to consider it a representative of the progressive forces of history, that in a perspective of a situation of war, as Gramsci states, "it means obtaining a part of the results of a victorious war without having to fight." Therefore, the most important challenge for China to become a truly worldwide hegemonic power is to consolidate its position as a leader and guide of a system of alliances beyond the deployment of the Belt and Road Initiative. That means that restricted State should give way to full State in order to project a new common sense to the

[2] One of the main goals is to connect the East Asia economic circle at one end with the developed European economic circle at the other, to mobilize the economic potential of the inland countries (ACCA, 2017). In this way, during 2019, the China–Europe freight train ran 8225 trains in 18 countries and 57 cities on the European continent.

world. Definitely, post-pandemic COVID-19 world will take to a spike in the clash of development pathways mainly between neoliberalism and Chinese competitive State, but the final outline of the new World Order to come will last depend on the class struggle.

References

ACCA. (2017). *The belt and road initiative: Reshaping the global value chain*. London: ACCA.

Beaubien, J. (2020, 26 de marzo). How South Korea reined in the outbreak without shutting everything down. *NPR*. Recovered from https://www.npr.org/sections/goatsandsoda/2020/03/26/821688981/how-south-korea-reigned-in-the-outbreak-without-shutting-everything-down.

Clarke, H. (2020, March 16). Is UK's coronavirus 'herd immunity' plan a deadly gamble? *South China Morning Post*. Recovered from https://www.scmp.com/news/world/europe/article/3075368/uks-coronavirus-herd-immunity-plan-deadly-gamble.

Lewis, L. (2020, 21 de abril). Coronavirus crisis may finally prove that 'Japan Inc' does not exist. *Financial Times*. Recovered from https://www.ft.com/content/04b43782-1ab8-437e-9b6e-4c1f43324b76.

Pesek, W. (2020, 20 de abril). Japan's leader is following a Trumpian playbook on the coronavirus. *The Washington Post*. Recovered from https://www.washingtonpost.com/opinions/2020/04/20/japans-leader-is-following-trumpian-playbook-coronavirus/.

Rhodes, A., Ferdinande, P., Flaatten, H., Guidet, B., Metnitz, P., & Moreno, R. (2012). The variability of critical care bed numbers in Europe. *Intensive Care Med* 38, 1647–1653. https://doi.org/10.1007/s00134-012-2627-8. Recovered from https://link.springer.com/content/pdf/10.1007/s00134-012-2627-8.pdf.

Sánchez, C. (2020, April 30). Crise da saúde e contradição neoliberal na fronteira norte do México: propostas de solução desde abaixo e baseadas na economia social do conhecimento. *Boletim. No. 18. Instituto de Pesquisa e Planejamento Urbano e Regional. Universidade Federal do Rio de Janeiro*. Recovered from http://ippur.ufrj.br/index.php/pt-br/noticias/outros-eventos/716-crise-da-saude-e-contradicao-neoliberal-na-fronteira-norte-do-mexico-propostas-de-solucao-desde-abaixo-e-baseadas-na-economia-social-do-conhecimento.

Sánchez, C. (2016). The challenge of incorporating Mexico into the TPP in Knowledge Capitalism surpassing its integration into NAFTA. *Economía Informa, 400*, 40–66. https://doi.org/10.1016/j.ecin.2016.09.004.

SCMP. (2020, 26 de marzo). Europe's coronavirus lockdown nightmare. *South China Morning Post*. Recovered from https://multimedia.scmp.com/infogr

aphics/news/world/article/3077057/europe-coronavirus/index.html?src=article-launcher.

USA Facts. (2020, May 1). *Coronavirus locations: COVID-19 map by county and state*. Recovered from https://usafacts.org/visualizations/coronavirus-covid-19-spread-map/.

CHAPTER 8

Conclusion: New Cold War as Post-pandemic COVID-19 World Order?

The world had not yet been overcome the consequences of the global productive financial crisis of 2008 on the national and regional economies when it faced the pandemic crisis which economic repercussions have yet to be fully observed. Although States that undertook a neoliberal development pathway carried out attempts to revitalize their economies after the financial crisis through monetary policy instruments qualified as innovative, recovery of the pace of economic growth in developed economies is in doubt today more than ever.

Furthermore, these efforts to revive a declining economic activity on both sides of the Atlantic still focus on the financial sphere through the stock exchanges, as transmission mechanisms with the productive sectors. No alternative proposals present so far to give a new impulse to the economies through strategies that directly influence the most dynamic industrial branches of the current phase of development. In addition, the slowdown in the pace of Chinese economic growth, as well as the shift toward strengthening its domestic market to overcome the depressed conditions of its foreign export markets, imposes a new outlook and challenges to come for the world economy, particularly for developing countries and specially for Latin America.

C. M. Sánchez Ramírez, *Knowledge Capitalism and State Theory*, Palgrave Insights into Apocalypse Economics,
https://doi.org/10.1007/978-3-030-71411-6_8

Between the burst of the.com bubble (2002) and the market failure (2008), developing economies grew four percent points more than developed ones in average. This was a significant expansion period for Latin America economy, sustained by a high demand for raw materials and primary products by East Asian countries, meaning an average growth rate of 3.7% for the region. This was slightly higher than the region's average growth during the seventies, when countries like Brazil were in the final stage of exports substituting as national industrialization strategy. Moreover, this was clearly higher than the economic decline of −0.8% during the eighties and the subsequent tenuous recovery during the period of greatest commitment of the region to neoliberalism in the nineties of the twentieth century, when it presented an average growth rate of 1.8%.

With the end of the boom period after 2008 and the worsening of the economic perspective resulting from COVID-19 pandemic, it becomes clear the inability of the dominant theoretical paradigm (monetarist, new classical macroeconomics, Keynesianism of the neoclassical synthesis and the Austrian school) to relaunch the productive sphere to a new stage of expansion. Therefore, in the face of collapse and uncertainty, an institutional rearrangement is necessary to provide new solutions to the crisis situation, taking into account the material conditions of the present phase of development, not only from the market sphere, but also from the State as representative of the social interest.

The revisit of the literature that addresses the theory of the State in an integral perspective is the theoretical challenge of the present work. There are few theoretical bodies approaching the State theory beyond economics and politics, but also considering its space-time dimensions. Gramsic's conceptual framework around Historic Bloc—Hegemony—and full State provides the needed backbone to carry out this integral effort. As a State form resulted from hegemonic capability within Historic Bloc implies a spatial dimension, it also characterized by its time dimension in terms of the phase of development of the capitalist mode of production. Moreover, a phase of development not only considers capitalism long-term cyclicality, but also the articulation between economic structure and social fabric mediated by the hegemonic capability within the Historic Bloc. That is to say, evolving State-spatial-forms over time.

This theoretical device enables a set of approach lenses to analyze the national experiences of developed and developing countries that undertook alternative development pathways to neoliberalism in Knowledge Capitalism, as well as assess the recent search efforts of post-neoliberal development pathways in South America. Currently, distinctive State-spatial forms constitute without its distinctive features fully defined, outlined in this work as Innovate or Competitive States depending on studied national experiences, and which in turn are in a constant transformation imposed by an accelerated socio-spatial dynamics in this phase of development.

The study cases of Finland and China show that there are possibilities of overcoming the condition of backwardness and this option is viable outside the dominant neoliberal pathway. The Finnish Innovate State undertook a development pathway through conception and design of products linked to the most dynamic industrial branches of the current phase, in the chains of high cognitive value added. Meanwhile, Chinese Competitive State took advantage of its abundant labor force combined with a restrictive wage policy to initially integrate into the lower and middle links of value chains of the inter-industrial and global division of labor, adapting its labor force to the requirements of flexibility in production, but constantly ascending in global value chains.

A time lag in which different groups and social fractions within both Historic Blocs weaved agreements and alliances around a new development project explains the differential insertion of both States in Knowledge Capitalism. While toward the second half of the previous century, Finland had relatively mature Gramscian institutions resulted from a strong consensus capability within its Historic Bloc, and China began the reconfiguration of its Bloc two decades before the new century. This difference between both national experiences also expressed in different levels of consensus and coercion in their ruling classes hegemonic capability. In Finland, full State tends to prevail resulting from a high consensus capability of ruling classes to the subaltern ones around the historic project of a society of innovation and learning. Meanwhile, in China, restricted State prevails, with a strong coercion capability of ruling classes to different fractions of bureaucracy and civil society.

In the current transition of Chinese development pathway accelerated by COVID-19 pandemic to an inwards growth model, the Competitive State challenge is to move toward an Innovate State, encouraging the formation of growing endogenous knowledge circuits that allow it to position itself at the forefront in the design of products with high cognitive value added. This is to overcome dependence on the absorption capacity of its products by mature foreign markets, becoming effectively and not only potentially in the world's largest consumer market. Moreover, moving to a society of innovation as an internal strategy combined with Belt & Road Initiative as an external one could together significantly alter the global and inter-industrial division of labor configuration, thus transferring the epicenter of the global economy from Atlantic to Pacific, finishing U.S Hegemony.

Latin America must prepare for this scenario. Therefore, it is essential to relaunch and upgrade alternative development pathways to neoliberalism undertook in South America at the beginning of the new century. Transition to post-neoliberalism in Latin America requires a new agreement, overcoming the condition of historical crisis of Hegemony within Historic Blocs, in a perspective of progress under the economic–structural conditions of this phase of development. Brazil and Argentina made the most advanced but still insufficient efforts in South America driven by neo-developmental States. Both achieved important social advances particularly in reducing poverty, as well as deploying physical and energy infrastructure that increased their competitiveness. However, strong ties remain between the agro-mining exporter and landlord bourgeoisies with international financial capital, meaning an anchor to neoliberalism, which up to now has neutralized the pulse of massive social mobilizations that let the State to obtain an embedded autonomy to lead an alternative development pathway. Thus, neo-developmental States periods in Brazil and Argentina derived in a wasted decade for overcoming backwardness in the region.

Obtaining lessons from Innovate and Competitive States to build a new Hegemony in Latin America through a neo-developmental State-spatial action should consider first a new role for Central Banks to regulate national financial systems in order to protect the economies from speculative international financial torrents. Second, promotion of development banking in strategic economic sectors of the economy, particularly those linked to the electronic and telecommunications driving industries, prioritizing areas where competitive advantages already exist. Third, promotion of industrial association and collaboration programs to build forward and backward linkages between national and foreign industries, as well as articulation between local and global scales but under national development goals. Fourth, promotion of innovation, learning and creative societies through education, culture and research and development increasing budgets together with the deployment of telecommunications infrastructure and its wide access.

Finally, the evolving State-spatial forms are currently in a boiling process expressed in a global clash of predominant development pathways deepened by financial-productive crisis of 2008 and pandemic emergency of 2020. The electoral dispute in the United States in 2020 that resulted in Joe Biden as the 46th President of the U.S. will involve the reorientation of the neoliberal development pathway through consensus, incorporating the economic and political interests of social fractions that remained in a subordinate position during the rise of Knowledge Capitalism. This reorientation of neoliberalism initiated by Trump through coercion as a result of social questioning after the market failure and that Biden will necessarily have to maintain through consensus could mean the integration of elements of the Finnish Innovate State to confront the Chinese Competitive State from a Keynesian neoliberalism. The return of the State in the United States in the face of China's strength in Knowledge Capitalism could reproduce the rise of the Welfare State in the face of the growing influence of the USSR that took place during Fordism-Keynesianism, shaping a New Cold War as a prelude to post pandemic COVID-19 World Order.

Index

C. M. Sánchez Ramírez, *Knowledge Capitalism and State Theory*, Palgrave Insights into Apocalypse Economics, https://doi.org/10.1007/978-3-030-71411-6

C

D

E

The manufacturer's authorised representative in the EU is Springer Nature Customer Service Centre GmbH, Europaplatz 3, 69115 Heidelberg, Germany. If you have any concerns regarding our products, please contact ProductSafety@springernature.com

Printed and bound by CPI Group (UK) Ltd, Croydon, CR0 4YY

30/09/2026

02225475-0019